THE·DEGREES OF·THE SOUL

Classics of Muslim Spirituality, 5

Also available in this series:

1 Imām ʿAbdallāh al-Ḥaddād, *The Book of Assistance.* (1989)
2 Ḥabīb Aḥmad Mashhūr al-Ḥaddād, *Key to the Garden.* (1990)
3 Imām ʿAbdallāh al-Ḥaddād, *The Lives of Man.* (1991)
4 Imām ʿAbdallāh al-Ḥaddād, *Gifts for the Seeker.* (1992)

THE·DEGREES OF·THE SOUL

SPIRITUAL STATIONS ON THE SUFI PATH

SHAYKH ABD AL-KHALIQ AL-SHABRAWI

TRANSLATED FROM THE ARABIC BY
MOSTAFA AL-BADAWI

THE QUILLIAM PRESS
1997

First published 1997 (1417) by
The Quilliam Press Ltd.,
80 Lamble Street,
London NW5 4AB

ISBN 1 872038 12 3 (cloth)
ISBN 1 872038 13 1 (paper)

Arabic title: *Marātib al-nafs*

British Library Cataloguing in Publication Data.
A catalogue record for this book is available
from the British Library

Printed and bound in Great Britain by
Redwood Books Ltd., Trowbridge, Wiltshire

CONTENTS

TRANSLATOR'S INTRODUCTION

The aim of religion is to reunite man with his Creator. Reunion occurs in Paradise, once the believing servants are safely past the dangerous events that follow the Resurrection, so that God bestows upon them, each according to his degree, the supreme reward: the beatific vision of His Countenance. For the elite, however, the thought of reunion has more immediate implications, since they are the fortunate few who need not wait until they enter the Garden to experience the delight of that vision; for they are given to enter the inward Garden of direct knowledge while still in this world. This is the highest purpose of man's existence, and the way to achieve it is consequently the most precious thing that anyone may wish to learn. Hence at the heart of every revealed religion there exists a central core representing its profoundest and most precious aspect, namely those teachings and practices which together carry the seeker beyond theoretical knowledge and up the spiritual ladder to the direct experience of the Divine Presence.

The core of Islam, its central and most profound aspect, is called Sufism, which is that method of spiritual realization whose doctrinal and ritual supports are those of Islam. Thus there can be no true understanding of Islam without at least some degree of understanding of Sufism; neither can there be any real understanding of Sufism separately from Islam, nor is it possible to have a form of Sufism lying outside the boundaries of Islam. An Islam without Sufism would be a body without a heart, a body deprived of that which pulsates within it and suffuses it with life; while a Sufism outside Islam would be a heart without a body, an organ deprived of the material support upon which its own life depends. Just as the body and the heart depend entirely on each other for survival, so do Islam and Sufism stand in relation to each other. This is clearly demonstrated by the fact that the most celebrated Sufis have typically been reputable orthodox scholars, a pattern which has been maintained to this day. The efforts of certain orientalists to cast doubt on the provenance of Sufism and their attempts to ascribe to it an origin foreign to Islam are inevitable and their motives obvious. Being unable or unwilling to acknowledge the truth that the most profound aspects of any doctrine must be impossible to grasp from the outside, they are victims of the spirit of our times, which has led a whole civilization to labour under the delusion that anything at all can be understood by reading about it and subjecting it to a 'rational' evaluation ('rational' here meaning conforming with the idiosyncrasies and prejudices of that same civilization). Less obvious, but also less excusable, are the motives of those Muslims who, themselves lacking all spiritual aptitude, cannot bear to see it in others and thus proceed to deny and combat it with surprising vehemence. The first represent an attempt to undermine Islam from without, and the second, its no less inevitable complement, the assault from within. Both would feel much more comfortable with a dry, unidimensional Islam requiring from its adherents no more than the shallowest doctrinal understanding and a correspondingly superficial ritual conformity allowing no room at all for the quest for inner purity and enlightenment. This process leaves in the end nothing but an empty shell, a mere form devoid of all meaning. None of the great religions has been spared these assaults, for these are nothing but the inevitable and thus predictable response of the lower worlds to the light descending from above. The stratagems used during the various phases of such wars are innumerable, and we shall perhaps have the opportunity to discuss them in detail in another context.

Once a religion loses its power to reunite people with their Lord, experientially and in this life, it becomes simply a matter of time before its vitality dwindles further to the extent that it also loses its power of salvation and then disintegrates. Left behind are no more than valueless fragments resembling those of a broken mirror, the pieces of which are so small that they are no longer capable of fulfilling their original purpose, yet are still identifiable as parts of that particular mirror and hence of being claimed as operative parts of the original. This is the situation of the modern West following the disintegration of Christianity.

One of the major proofs that a religion still nurtures its living, pulsating heart is the presence within its fold of the finished product of its realizatory method, namely the 'arriver', the saint who has entered the Divine Presence and has thus become capable of guiding others along the same route. These are those human beings in whom the Adamic potential for sainthood and gnosis has become actualized. Their presence being the irrefutable criterion of the vitality of any given religion, it is not only the manifest failure of the Christian world to produce a single gnostic for centuries, but also its loss of the knowledge of the method to do so, that has led so many Muslims to regard Christianity as irretrievably defunct. In contrast, such 'arrivers' abound in the Muslim world and are still relatively easy to find despite the spiritual bankruptcy of a majority immersed in crude physical pursuits and dazzled by the material expertise of the West, and despite the efforts of most Sufis to remain in obscurity in such a hostile climate.

In the context of Sufism, Imām al-Ḥaddād placed people in one of three categories when he wrote in *Gifts for the Seeker*: 'Every human being is either a traveller, an arriver, or a non-traveller'. By 'non-travellers' he obviously refers to the heedless Muslim majority, but this may be extended to include the non-Muslims. The present volume, being an exposition of the stages of spiritual realization by a master who has completed the entire journey successfully and also taken innumerable disciples through it, must arouse in anyone with the slightest spiritual inclination a yearning for the return to God. To be spiritually inclined is to feel, however vaguely and discontinuously, that there must be something beyond the material world, that to take this world at face value cannot possibly be the ultimate purpose of a human being, that there must be meaning within every form, that there must be some way in which those meanings can be grasped - in short, that there is something in man that requires more than mere animal survival, something capable of reaching for the Absolute. A clear and detailed exposition of the path such as this volume offers, when it meets with such an inclination, renders the path and its ultimate goal intelligible, sets the very idea of spiritual realization within the range of the conceivable, and brings home the urgency and immediate feasibility of such an endeavour. In other words, the journey toward infinite reality takes on much more substance in one's mind, and this may be followed by the thought that it is, after all, not unreasonable to desire such a thing. This may induce those with little or no previous knowledge of such matters to seek to know more, and hence the beginning is reached. As for those who are already in possession of adequate theoretical knowledge on the subject but perceive the practical aspect as remote and unrealizable, they may be driven to give it much more serious consideration and perhaps actively begin the search for those able to throw more light on it for them, or perhaps, more decisively, for the master who will accept them as disciples. There are two other kinds of non-travellers who may draw much benefit from this volume: those who are actually affiliated to Sufism but are still unaware of its deeper implications and possibilities, and those who tend to confuse book knowledge with realization, that is, the purely mental assimilation of doctrine with inspiration and gnosis. Both will find here landmarks and criteria which, if honestly applied, will allow them a clear assessment of their situation and its requirements.

For travellers, the value of this work lies in its explicit description of certain points of importance that previous masters had hitherto left implicit, drawing on the deep insights of the Khalwatī perspective, as well as in the schematic organization of material that would have had to be gleaned from dozens of older treatises. Masters write only from inspiration; indeed the author of the present volume stated to one of his close disciples that his pen ran swifter than his hand as he was writing it, and each treatise is a response to the needs of its times. The need to schematise arises from the deterioration that has befallen the powers of assimilation of the Muslim nation. A delicate balance has to be maintained between the quest for intelligibility and the need to avoid the excessive rigidity and constriction likely to be imposed by schematisation on knowledge that is by its very nature fluid and open-ended. It is often forgotten that Sufism is essentially an oral tradition; no book is therefore likely to obviate the need for the oral teaching, guidance, and constant supervision of a master. Each master will use the terminology proper to the school to which he belongs, and the same term is therefore likely to signify more than one thing according to who is using it. This is why the author has provided precise definitions for each term he uses, which should leave the reader in no doubt as to the intended meaning and also allow him or her to compare them with similar or equivalent terms in other works. In his introduction he explains how he intends the terms 'soul' (*nafs*), 'spirit' (*rūḥ*), and 'secret' (*sirr*) to be understood, since other authors use them differently.

The book provides an account of the various 'ailments' of the soul and their remedies. The ailments constitute the veils which prevent the Eye of the Heart from beholding the Unseen, while the remedies are the various devotional and self-disciplining practices that unpick such veils until such time as the first glimmer of light shines through. From there the practices lead upward, step by step, until human perfection is achieved, which is the completion of the journey. There are dangers on the way. Novices may come to believe with the first flash of light that they have become great saints. More advanced wayfarers may develop the illusion that they have reached the end of the path and have now become masters and guides in their own right. In both instances, as in cases of severe breach of spiritual courtesy, the traveller may be dispossessed of whatever gains he has achieved and find himself plummeting to a level lower than he could ever have imagined. The length of the chapters indicates which audience the author wishes to address, for as the book progresses the chapters become briefer, until those concerned with the last three stages are no more than two or three pages each. This is because those who have already travelled as far as the highest three degrees are hardly in need of systematic treatises, and one suspects that the shaykh has written these chapters simply so as not to leave the work incomplete, to give novices an inkling of the nature of the higher reaches of spiritual realization and perhaps to provide a few subtle indications to be understood only by wayfarers who are approaching those levels.

The author of this treatise is the Sufi shaykh and Shāfiʿī scholar ʿAbd al-Khāliq al-Shabrāwī, a descendant of the second caliph ʿUmar ibn al-Khaṭṭāb, may God be pleased with him, through his father, and of Imām al-Ḥusayn, may God be pleased with him, through his mother. His paternal grandfather was the distinguished shaykh ʿUmar al-Shabrāwī, eminent scholar, lecturer at Al-Azhar University, saint, Sufi master, and founder of the Shabrāwī off-shoot of the Khalwatī Sufi order (*ṭarīqa*). He was one of those exceptional individuals who are born with a purity of soul sufficient to qualify them for a swift ascent of the spiritual ladder and an early blossoming of sainthood. Shaykh ʿUmar al-Shabrāwī was a man of great presence and charisma who attracted a multitude of disciples, many of whom became famous masters during his life-time and after his death. He was succeeded at the head of the order by his son, ʿAbd al-Salām, who died four years later, in his early thirties, to be succeeded after an interval by ʿAbd al-Salām's own son ʿAbd al-Khāliq.

Shaykh ʿAbd al-Khāliq was born in 1887 in a small town north of Cairo during his grandfather's life and grew up 'under his solicitous gaze', which is the Sufi way of saying that he received intense spiritual attention from him. So intense was this, indeed, that many members of the family were baffled; but the shaykh's response to this was to tell them: 'Leave me alone with my grandson, for I see in him and know of his future what you can neither see nor know. This is the bearer of the order's flag after me!' The author was still a child when Shaykh ʿUmar died, followed by his son ʿAbd al-Salām. However, he followed the family tradition, committed the Noble Qur'ān to memory, then joined Al-Azhar University to study under the foremost authorities of his time. His teachers were unanimous in giving him great respect and consideration despite his youth, and many of them predicted a great future for him when he graduated in 1914. During the following years he was known to keep regular night vigils and remain in constant remembrance of God.

He taught at Al-Azhar for a few years, refusing to take charge of the *ṭarīqa* and preferring to remain in obscurity. He had also received the Shādhilī and Naqshbandī *ṭarīqas* through his grandfather and other masters but, to protect his intimacy with his Lord, chose to remain aloof despite repeated requests from the *ṭarīqa*'s affiliates that he administer the oath of allegiance to them and become their guide. Eventually they approached his uncle, who was one of the order's guides, and implored him to convince the shaykh to accept their allegiance. His uncle, the gnostic shaykh ʿUthmān al-Shabrāwī addressed him thus: 'The brothers are numerous and I have grown old and am no longer able to carry this burden.' At first, Shaykh ʿAbd al-Khāliq refused, but seeing the old man's insistence his heart softened and he finally consented to take over as master of the order. Soon the number of affiliates grew and his fame spread. This led him to resign his Azhar teaching post and accept another as imām of the al-Fatḥ mosque, which allowed him more time to devote to his disciples. He spent the remainder of his life teaching, disciplining, refining, and guiding people along the path.

One of his disciples described him as 'a mentor of exceptional quality, a guide to the path of the Truth whose style was ever courteous. He protected his disciples from all tiring and wearisome things: whenever a spiritual state threatened to overwhelm a disciple he would bring him to a halt, and whenever a disciple surrendered to indolence, the neglect of his acts of worship, and the attraction of his appetites, the Shaykh would take him by the hand and make him move ...'. Among those who travelled the path under his guidance were his brother ʿAbd al-Salām and his son Muṣṭafā. The latter became the order's master at the death of the shaykh in 1947. He was an eminent scholar of sufficient authority to have held the office of deputy Grand-Muftī of Egypt. Before his death in 1994 he was gracious enough to permit us to publish this book both in its original Arabic and in translation.

MOSTAFA AL-BADAWI
al-Madīna al-Munawwara, 1415

THE DEGREES OF THE SOUL

Author's Prologue

In the name of God, the Merciful and Compassionate

THE PASSIONAL SOUL [*al-nafs al-shahwāniyya*] is that subtle vapour that exists behind life, sensory perception, and voluntary movements. This is what the philosophers called 'vital spirit'. It is an essence whose influence shines upon the body. When this influence involves both the body's outward and inward aspects,[1] the result is the waking state. When it involves the inward of the body but not the outward, sleep results. When its effect is interrupted altogether, death occurs. (And glorified be the Wise Maker!)

The Rational Soul [*al-nafs al-nāṭiqa*] is an essence which in itself is unrelated to matter, but is connected to it inasmuch as it acts upon it. This soul is that which is termed either 'Inciting', 'Reproachful', 'Inspired', 'Serene', 'Contented', 'Found Pleasing', or 'Perfect'. Whenever it acquires an attribute it also acquires the name that designates it. When it befriends the abovementioned passional soul and submits to it it is called 'Inciting' [to evil] [*ammāra bi'l-sū'*].[2] When it submits to the dictates of *sharīᶜa* and agrees to follow the truth but still harbours some attraction to passional pleasures it is called 'Reproachful' [*lawwāma*].[3] When this attraction disappears, and it acquires strength in opposing the passional soul and is attracted to the World of Sanctity [*ᶜālam al-quds*][4] and begins to receive inspirations, it is then called 'Inspired' [*mulhama*].[5] When its agitation quietens and the passional soul loses all power over it and it forgets its pleasures altogether it is termed 'Serene' [*muṭma'inna*]. When it ascends higher than this and the [spiritual] stations themselves lose importance in its sight and it becomes extinct to all [its own] wishes it is called 'Contented' [*rāḍiya*]. When this state increases, it is termed 'Found Pleasing' [*marḍīya*], that is, to both the Real and created beings.[6] When it is commanded to return to created beings to guide and perfect them it is called 'Perfect' [*kāmila*].[7] We shall provide you with a description of each type of soul in the chapter devoted to it, together with its signs, attributes, states, world, qualities (whether praiseworthy or blameworthy), the supernatural happenings that the seeker may experience as he develops through each of them, the invocations specific to each of them, and other matters that you shall come upon in detail, God willing.

Know that the essence which we have mentioned and termed the Rational Soul has other appellations, for it is also termed the 'heart', the 'subtle human faculty', and the 'reality of man'. It is that which is aware and knows, and to which legal and moral commandments are addressed. This essence has an outward aspect, which is the aforementioned passional soul, and an inward aspect which is the Spirit [*rūḥ*]. Its inward aspect itself has an inward aspect, which is the 'Secret' [*sirr*]. The Secret has its own inward aspect, which is the 'Secret of the Secret' [*sirr al-sirr*]. The Secret of the Secret in its turn has an inward aspect, which is the 'Hidden' [*khafā'*]. The Hidden has its own inward aspect, which is the 'Most Hidden' [*al-akhfā*].

The 'inward' of a thing is its reality and substance. The inward, and the inward of the inward, may be rendered clearer by an example. The inward of a bed, for instance, is pieces of wood, the inward of these is trees, the inward of the trees is the four elements,[8] and the inward of these is primordial matter [*hāyūlā*]. So understand! Now that you know this, know that this singular Divine 'thing' is called, when at its most subtle and imperceptible, the 'Most Hidden'. When it descends one degree and becomes denser it is called the 'Hidden'. When it descends a second degree and becomes even denser it is called the 'Secret of the Secret', then in the same manner it becomes the 'Secret', then the 'Spirit'. Then it becomes the 'Heart', the 'Rational Soul', the 'Subtle Human Faculty', and 'Man'; for in this last degree it has four names. When it descends one further degree it becomes 'Bestial Man', or the 'Inciting Soul'.

Know that the purpose of travelling the Sufi path is to raise this Divine 'thing' step by step to its original degree by the use of the treatments and remedies prescribed by the most perfect among perfect men, the spirit of all guides, may God's blessings and peace be upon him.[9] These are: fasting, night vigils, restraint in speech, compassion for created beings, remembrance [*dhikr*], reflection [*fikr*], living on permitted [*ḥalāl*] and avoiding forbidden [*ḥarām*] things, and other treatments that will be dealt with in more detail later, God willing. This should be done without exceeding the legal limits, not even by an atom, since the one who takes remedies other than those of *sharīʿa* will not cure himself of his sickness but, on the contrary, will increase in sickness upon sickness.

When the wayfarer, the seeker of perfection, is at the lowest degree, by which I mean that of Bestial Man, and his soul is one that is Inciting [to evil], then the remedy by which he can ascend to the degree of the Heart is *Lā ilāha illa'Llāh*. He must constantly use this invocation, loudly and forcefully, to awaken himself from distraction. When the wayfarer is at the degree of the Heart, then his remedy, which will raise him to the degree of the Spirit, is to eat sparingly, sleep sparingly, and use the invocation *Allāh* in abundance. We shall discuss in the following chapters the remedies that a wayfarer on the path needs in order to ascend from one degree to another until he reaches the place from whence he had [originally] descended, that is, the Adamic form which was the *qibla* of the angels.[10] And know that although the *ḥadīth*s which have been handed down condemning the world and worldly people are innumerable, still, those who love the world and strain for its pleasures profit neither from those *ḥadīths* nor from anything else. Those who love God are the enemies of His enemy, which is the world [*dunyā*], for He has not given it a second glance since He created it. The fortunate man is he who knows what he was created for and prepares for it, shuns all else, and seeks of worldly things no more than his necessary needs. The unfortunate is he who is overcome by passional desires and by distraction so that he is ever striving for more food, clothes and pleasures. *And power and ability are only by God, the Exalted, the Great.*

INTRODUCTION

An encouragement to take the path of Sufism, the merits of the path, and how to free oneself from vices

Know that to quest for perfection is a most noble quality. 'Perfection' here means to divest oneself of blameworthy attributes and adorn oneself with praiseworthy ones. The blameworthy attributes are: ignorance, irascibility, rancour, resentful envy, avarice, pride, arrogance, conceit, illusion, ostentation, the love of prestige and power, excessive volubility and jesting affectation, boastfulness, levity, disruption of social bonds, prying into the privacy of others, [long] hopes, greed, and bad character. The praiseworthy attributes are these: knowledge, forbearance, inward purity, generosity, meekness, gentleness, humility, patience, gratitude, renunciation, reliance on God, love, yearning, modesty, contentment, sincerity, truthfulness, vigilance, self-scrutiny, reflection, concern and compassion for other creatures, to love or detest solely for God, deliberation in all matters, weeping and feeling grieved, wishing for obscurity and seclusion, guilelessness, being of good counsel and few words, awe and submission, and possessing a broken heart and a good character.

The purpose of travelling the Sufi path is the acquisition of perfection and freedom from repulsive traits, a process which is required and commanded by *Sharīʿa*.

Irascibility [*ghaḍab*]

Freeing oneself from irascibility is required because the Prophet, may blessings and peace be upon him, has said: 'No-one becomes angry without drawing closer to the brink of hell.' And Abū Hurayra,[11] may God be pleased with him, related that a man once said: 'O Messenger of God, tell me of a deed I should do, even if small.' He was told: 'Do not be angry!' And Ibn Masᶜūd,[12] may God be pleased with him, said that the Messenger of God, may God's blessings and peace be upon him, once asked them: 'Whom do you consider the strongest among you?' They replied: 'The one whom others cannot defeat.' But he said: 'It is not so; it is the one who controls himself when angry.'

The outward appearance of the angry person is ugly enough, yet his inner appearance is uglier still. Irascibility is a reprehensible attribute that is caused by the agitation of the blood in the heart as it demands revenge. Its opposite is forbearance, which one must impose upon oneself initially until such time as it becomes habitual. The Prophet, may blessings and peace be upon him, said: 'Knowledge is gained by learning, and forbearance is gained by imposing it [on oneself]. The one who chooses the good shall be given it and the one who avoids evil shall come to be protected from it.' And he said, may God's blessings and peace be upon him: 'Seek knowledge, and seek with knowledge serenity and forbearance. Be gentle with those whom you teach and those from whom you learn. Do not act tyrannically lest your ignorance defeat you.'[13] And he said to his Companions: 'Seek elevation in God's sight!' 'And what is that, O Messenger of God?' they asked, and he replied: 'To preserve your bonds with those who sever theirs with you, to give to those who withhold from you, and to be forbearing with those who mistreat you.' And there are many other *ḥadīths* condemning anger and praising forbearance.

To rid oneself entirely of blameworthy anger and acquire praiseworthy forbearance to the extent that it becomes habitual is only possible if one takes the Sufi path, for through it the power of anger is broken and it comes under the sovereignty of reason and the law, so that it becomes subdued and under control. When such a person becomes angry it will be solely for the sake of God, and anger for the sake of God is an exalted rank which is possible only for those who have reached in their ascent the fourth degree, that of the Serene Soul. Those who claim it for themselves but have yet to reach this degree are liars who confuse truth with falsehood. ᶜAlī,[14] may God be pleased with him, once said: 'The Prophet, may God's blessings and peace be upon him, never became angry for worldly reasons,' meaning that he became angry only for the sake of God the Exalted, 'and when he became angry for the truth none would recognise him,' meaning that he became unrecognisable because of the power of his anger in support of the truth and for the defeat of falsehood.

Resentful Envy [*ḥasad*]

This is another repugnant attribute, which can be completely removed only by taking the Sufi path in the manner that we shall describe in the following chapters. The Prophet, may blessings and peace be upon him, said: 'Resentful envy consumes good deeds just as fire consumes firewood.' Resentful envy occurs when a person hates to see the favours that God has bestowed on his brother and wishes him to lose them. But when he neither hates to see them in his brother's possession nor wishes him to lose them, but simply wishes to possess the same himself, this is called ordinary envy and is not reprehensible. The Prophet, may blessings and peace be upon him, said: 'The believer envies, but the hypocrite resents.' And God's saying (Exalted is He!), *Wish not for what God has given some of you in preference to others*, [4:32] means that you should not wish these same favours to be yours to the exclusion of others. [This is the meaning,] since it is not reprehensible to wish for similar favours, but neither is it commendable. This relates to worldly things, whereas in religious matters it is in fact commendable [to desire the same favours].

Rancour [*ḥiqd*]

This too is repugnant, since it leads to resentful envy, shunning, hatred, disruption of relationships, and prying into the privacy of those who are the objects of that rancour.

The Prophet, may blessings and peace be upon him, said: 'It is not permissible for a Muslim man to shun his brother for more than three [days]. The one who does so and then dies, enters the Fire.'

And he said: 'Spy not on one another, resent not one another, hate not one another, turn not your backs on one another, and be, O servants of God, brothers!' And he said: 'The ailments of the previous nations have afflicted you: resentful envy and rancour. These are the Shavers. I do not say that they shave hair but they shave faith.' And Ibn ʿUmar,[15] may God be pleased with him, said: 'The Messenger of God, may God's blessings and peace be upon him, once climbed the pulpit and said in a loud voice: 'O you who have accepted Islam with your tongues but have not received faith in your hearts! Do not offend the Muslims! Abuse them not, nor pry into their privacies, seeking to shame them; for the one who pries into the privacy of his brother Muslim seeking to shame him, God shall pry into his privacy, and the one into whose privacy God pries He shall expose, even were he in the depths of his dwelling."'

However, you should know that shunning can [in some situations] be permissible for legally acceptable reasons.

Avarice [*bukhl*]

This has been condemned by God and His Messenger. God the Exalted has said: *And those who are protected from the avarice in themselves, they are those who succeed.* [59:9] And: *Let not those who withhold what God has given them of His favours think that it is better for them. Nay, it is worse for them. That which they withheld will be hung around their necks on the Day of Arising.* [3:180] And he said, may God's blessings and peace be upon him: 'Beware of avarice, for it has destroyed those who were before you; it made them spill blood and profane what is sacrosanct.' And: 'The generous person is close to God, remote from His torment, and close to me. He does not enter the fire and I am his companion. And the miserly person does not enter the garden, and his companion is Satan.' The reality of generosity is that you give away whatever is in excess of your needs. Altruism [*īthār*] is greater, for it is the highest degree in generosity. It is to give away money that you in fact need.

Arrogance [*kibr*]

This too is blameworthy. God the Exalted said: *I shall turn from My signs those who wax proud on the earth without right.* [7:146] And He said (Exalted is He!): *And disappointment came to every obstinate tyrant.* [14:15] And the Prophet said, may God's blessings and peace be upon him: 'He in whose heart lies an atom's weight of arrogrance shall not enter the Garden.' And God (High and Majestic is He!) said [in a *ḥadīth qudsī*]: 'Pride is My upper garment and Might My lower garment. Those who dispute with Me over one of them, I shall cast into the Fire.'

Arrogance is an attribute of the soul which arises from one's perception of oneself.

Conceit [*ʿujb*]

This is also among the blameworthy attributes. The Prophet, may God's blessing and peace be upon him, said: 'Three things are ruinous: avarice when obeyed, passion when followed, and the admiration of a man for himself.' The reality of conceit is that it is a kind of inward pride that occurs when a person imagines himself to possess some kind of perfection, whether of knowledge or of behaviour. A wayfarer who feels that conceit is entering him should reflect on those who died as disbelievers, having once been [fervent] worshippers, such as Balaam.[16] He should think of Satan and address his own soul thus: 'Do not be pleased with your work until you become certain that God has accepted it. How can you be pleased with something the acceptance of which remains uncertain?'

Delusion [*ghurūr*]

This is one of the causes of ruin. God the Exalted has said: *So let not the present life delude you, and let not the deluder delude you of God.* [31:33] Delusion is believing a thing to be different from what it really is, and the acceptance by the soul of whatever imaginary and obscure things accord with its whims. It is thus a form of ignorance.

There are many kinds of deluded people. Some harbour the illusion that because God is Magnanimous and Merciful, they can indulge in sins [with impunity]. God is undoubtedly Magnanimous and Merciful, but all the Qur'ān indicates that His Magnanimity and Mercy (Exalted is He!) take the form of His assistance to do good in the world. He says: *Whomsoever God wishes to guide, He expands his breast to Islam.* [6:125] Then there are those who harbour illusions concerning the piety of their fathers and ancestors and the success that God the Exalted had granted them, but do not reflect on His saying to Noah: *He is not of your family, that is a deed not righteous.* [11:46] Others delude themselves with merely dressing like the virtuous and the Sufis, thinking that Sufism is no more than wearing wool and patched robes. Others delude themselves by learning the sayings of the Sufis and their special expressions. Others still, under the influence of delusion, discard all shame and abandon all works. Yet others become deluded with whatever openings into gnosis they are granted and halt with them, imagining that they have arrived.

The states of the deluded are many; therefore a wayfarer should not allow himself to be deceived, nor should anything stop him, nor should he be satisfied with small things. He should pursue realization and certainty, and abandon suspect and passional matters, and perceive things as they are, for the machinations of the devil are many.

Ostentation [*riyā'*]

This is forbidden [*ḥarām*], since He has said (Exalted is He!): *Woe to those who pray and are distracted from their prayers, who are showing off.* [107:4–6] And: *So let the one who hopes to meet his Lord do good works and empartner none to his Lord in worship.* [18:110] And the Prophet has said, may God's blessings and peace be upon him: 'That which I fear most for you is the lesser idolatry [*al-shirk al-aṣghar*].' 'What is the lesser idolatry?' they asked, and he replied: 'Ostentation.' And God the Exalted, at the time of requiting His servants for their works, will say: 'Go to those you showed off for in the world; see if you will find your reward with them!'

Know that the ostentatious person doubtless wishes to have a high-ranking place in the hearts of the people, and this is what makes him behave thus. As for the seeker of the path to the Real, he must strive to lower his rank in the hearts of others. Far removed, therefore, are the ostentatious from the path of the Real.

Love of prestige and leadership [*ḥubb al-jāh wa'l-riyāsa*]
This blameworthy trait also obstructs the road to the Real. The Messenger of God, may God's blessings and peace be upon him, said: 'It is sufficient evil for a son of Adam - except those whom God the Exalted protects - to have people pointing their fingers at him, whether for religious or worldly reasons.' And ʿAlī,[14] may God be pleased with him, said: 'Seek modesty, not fame; raise not yourself, guard secrets and maintain silence. You will then be safe, gladdening the righteous, and spiting the corrupt.' And Ibrāhīm ibn Adham[17] said: 'A person who loves fame and renown lacks sincerity.'

Know that it is the love of fame that is blameworthy. As for fame and celebrity in themselves, they can be either praiseworthy or blameworthy. When the intention is to exalt oneself and disdain others, it is blameworthy, but when it is to guide and benefit them, it is undoubtedly praiseworthy and deserving of recompense. The renown of the Prophets and the Rightly-guided Caliphs is higher than any other, and yet they shall be recompensed for it. The hallmark of praiseworthy fame is that its possessor perceives it as a burden, so that when someone comes along who is capable of taking over from him and relieving him of the strain, he is happy and welcomes the opportunity and, far from resenting him, feels grateful toward him. In any case, as soon as the heart of the wayfarer leans toward the love of prestige and leadership, his path is barred. He must therefore relish obscurity and whatever conduces to it, and he must behave in such a manner as to prevent people from thinking much of him, so that whenever he is seen he is paid neither much attention nor consideration, nor does anyone return his greetings. This is the state of the sincere seeker.

Talking excessively [*kathrat al-kalām*]

This is blameworthy since it leads to forbidden [*ḥarām*] things, and to others which are discouraged [*makrūh*], such as mentioning one's previous sins, [discussing] women, arguing, mixing [with distracted people], rivalry, speaking with affectation, using rhymed prose, pretentiousness, insults, obscenity, cursing, levity exceeding the bounds of the legally permissible, mocking, jeering, divulging secrets, lying, backbiting, slandering, and other such forbidden things which involve delving into that which does not concern one. The peril of the tongue is fatal: nothing is more dangerous, for all villainy arises from it. This is why the Prophet, may God's blessings and peace be upon him, praised silence, commended it, and bade his Companions maintain it, saying: 'Silence is wisdom, but the silent are few.' And: 'The one who keeps silent will be saved.' And he said to Muʿādh ibn Jabal:[18] 'Are people cast into the Fire on their faces for anything other than the harvest of their tongues?' And Abū Bakr al-Ṣiddīq,[19] may God be pleased with him, was so anxious about slips of the tongue that he would place a pebble in his mouth to prevent himself from speaking. 'This is what has led me into places,' he used to say, indicating his tongue. And Ibn Masʿūd,[12] may God be pleased with him, had seen so much of the tongue's perils that he used to say: '*Allāhu Akbar*! There is nothing more deserving of imprisonment than the tongue!' And the Prophet, may God's blessings and peace be upon him, said: 'When I was made to journey by night[20] I passed by people who were tearing at their faces with their nails. I asked: "O Gabriel, who are these?" and he replied: "Those who backbite and slander people in what touches on their honour".'

Backbiting is to say of your brother that which would displease him if he were to hear it, even though it might be the truth, and whether it concerns his person, acts, words, religion, world, dress, house, mount, or anything else. When you say something concerning any of these things, and it is true, and you know that it would distress him were he to hear it, this is backbiting. If it is not true then it is calumny, which is even worse. It makes little difference whether the subject of these is present or absent.

The *ḥadīths* forbidding the tongue's diseases that we have mentioned are numerous, but those who are not influenced by the few will benefit nothing from the many.

And success is from God.

Levity [*mizāḥ*]

This brings death to the heart and is succeeded by a darkness. Were the wayfarer to know how greatly his state diminishes each time he jests he would never do it again. This is known by those whose inward is illuminated. As for the people of darkness, they do not sense the perils of jesting. He has said, may blessings and peace be upon him: 'Argue not with your brother, nor jest with him.' You might say that the Prophet, may blessings and peace be upon him, jested but spoke the truth; but you should know that you are incapable of that kind of jesting, and it will therefore be better for you to renounce it, exception being made for the few times when you feel extremely oppressed or heavy-hearted.

Preoccupation with one's appearance [*al-tazayyun li'l-khalq*]

Improving one's appearance for other people's sake distracts the wayfarer and obstructs him in his quest. For it requires the acquisition of clothes, the use of perfume, coiling the turban in the correct manner, and other such things which divert his attention from the remembrance of his Lord (August and Majestic is He!) and from presence [of the heart]. The true wayfarer needs to be nothing in the sight of others, lacking any importance in their hearts. To embellish one's appearance for their sake contradicts this. As for the guide [*murshid*], the one whom God the Exalted has entrusted with summoning creation to the Real, he must do nothing to detract from his status in the eyes of the people. Whenever he wished to go out of his house to meet his Companions, the Prophet, may blessings and peace be upon him, looked [at himself] in a mirror and tidied his turban and his hair. ʿĀ'isha,[21] may God be pleased with her, once asked him about this and he replied: 'God likes His bondsman to beautify his appearance for his brothers whenever he goes out to meet them.'

Boasting [*tafākhur*]

This trait is blameworthy and forbidden. The Prophet has said, may blessings and peace be upon him, 'God has revealed to me: "Be humble, let none praise himself over another, and let none oppress another!".' It is possible to boast about one's wealth, ancestors, devotions, or knowledge. Any such boasting is all blameworthy and vile, especially for the wayfarer, since he is seeking to realise servitude [*ʿubūdiyya*], and abandon his opposition to God's Lordship [*rubūbiyya*], and such boasting conflicts with this.

Laughter [*ḍaḥik*]

Laughing also brings a death to the heart, which is why the Prophet never laughed, may God's blessings and peace be upon him, but only smiled. To smile is acceptable and praiseworthy in the sight of God, His Messenger, and the people. Laughter causes the heart to die and is unbecoming of a wayfarer.

Long hopes and greed [*al-amal wa'l-ḥirs*]

Both are vile, and those who possess such attributes are remote from the presence of the Possessor of Majesty. Ibn ʿUmar,[15] may God be pleased with both of them, said: 'The Messenger of God, may blessings and peace be upon him, clutched me bodily and said: "Be in this world as a stranger or a wayfarer, and consider yourself as one of the people of the graves".' Ibn ʿUmar also said: 'The Messenger of God, may blessings and peace be upon him, once passed by as my mother and I were using clay to [repair] something. He asked, "What is this, ʿAbdallāh?" And I replied, "Something that we are repairing." He said, "The matter is swifter than that!", meaning that death is nearer than that.'

Bad character [*sū' al-khuluq*]

Bad character is blameworthy in the eyes of both God and people, whereas good character is considered praiseworthy by both. The Messenger of God, may blessings and peace be upon him, said: 'By Him in Whose hand is my soul, none shall enter the Garden save he whose character is good.' And he used to say in his prayers [*duʿā'*]: 'O God, improve my appearance and my character!'

Know that the blameworthy traits that we have just enumerated are only some of the vices that a man may harbour; for it is impossible to mention them all. However, the person who will travel the path in the manner that we shall expound in the coming chapters will rid himself of all vices, for the wayfarer, when sincere, uproots them from their very origin so that no trace whatsoever remains of them. In doing so he applies the remedies that, God willing, we shall expound. As for those who wish to rid themselves of them without travelling the path of the People [*al-qawm*], they are seeking the impossible. Now that you know this, you know what benefit is to be obtained from taking the path of the People, may God be pleased with them. But there is something else to be gained which is even greater and the true aim, and that is to reach the degrees of nearness to the Presence of the Lord. And God is the helper.

Know that when turned toward the body [and occupied] with luxuries, worldly pleasures, and the appetites of the self, the heart is covered with seventy veils. In this station the heart is called the Inciting Soul, for its attributes are blameworthy anger, rancour, resentful envy, arrogance, pride, conceit, illusion, bad character, and other evil traits which render it far distant from the presence of its Lord. This is not surprising, since following passions renders an honourable man lowly. It has been related that Zulaykhā said to Yūsuf,[22] upon whom be peace: 'O Yūsuf! Greed and passion make slaves out of kings, while fortitude and piety make kings out of slaves.' And he said to her: '*Whoever has piety and steadfastness; God shall not cause the reward of those who do good to be lost.*' [12:90] This is because the heart is by right the ruler of the body, and the body obeys its commands and prohibitions. When it is overpowered by passion the ruler becomes the subject, and the matter is inverted so that the king becomes a subjugated prisoner in the power of a dog or a tyrannical enemy. This is why when a man follows his gluttonous and passionate tendencies he sees himself in his dreams prostrating himself before a pig or an ass, and when he follows his irascible tendency he sees himself prostrating before a dog.

Know that when the heart forgets itself in that accursed condition and prolongs its sojourn there it comes to lose that property which is specific to it, namely the ability to concentrate on the Unseen. The loss of this property is what is expressed as 'blackness of the heart', or 'stamping' [*ṭabʿ*],[23] or 'that which covers' [*rayn*].[24] For the heart is as a mirror, and when it is clear of all rust and blemishes, one can behold things in it; but when it exists covered with rust, with nothing to polish it or protect it from rust, then that rust becomes deeply ingrained and may even penetrate its depth so that it becomes impossible to remove. This is what the Prophet meant, may blessings and peace be upon him, when he said: 'Hearts rust just as iron does.' They asked him: 'What is it that polishes it, O Messenger of God?' And he replied, 'The remembrance of death and the recitation of the Qur'ān.'

Let whosoever wishes to reach God the Exalted first enter from the gate of all gates, which is repentance. This is the first gate to be crossed by the servant when he seeks to enter the presence of nearness to the Exaltation of the Lord.

Know that repentance is an obligation, since God the Exalted says: *And repent unto God all together, O you believers!* [24:31] This is why it is the consensus of the Nation that repentance is a duty. The Prophet said, may God's blessings and peace be upon him, when inviting people to it: 'The one who repents from his sin is as the one who is sinless; repentance erases whatever has preceded it.' And: 'The penitent is dear to God.' And: 'God is more delighted with His slave's repentance when he repents than one of you whose riding camel was cut loose in the desert carrying his food and water; when he has lost hope [in retrieving] his camel he [suddenly] sees it standing beside him, he takes hold of its bridle and, in sheer exultation, says, "O God! You are my servant and I am your lord!", his error being due to his excessive exultation.' And: 'God accepts the repentance of His bondsman until he is gasping.'[25] The verses and *ḥadīth*s concerning repentance are almost beyond numbering.

Know that repentance is an immediately incumbent obligation, since the avoidance of sins and obedience to God are an unceasing duty. Al-Sanūsī[26] says that it is the consensus [*ijmāʿ*] that repentance should be immediate and that therefore its postponement multiplies the sins for those who do not repent. This is not the same as the multiplication of good deeds, for not to repent is itself a sin, so that failure to repent adds one sin upon another, the first being the original evil act and the second the absence of repentance. These two sins both require repentance, so that, if not forthcoming, they will become four according to the same pattern. This is multiplication, but not the same as the multiplication of good deeds, for God the Exalted says, *Whoso brings a good deed shall have ten the like thereof, and whoso brings an evil deed shall only be recompensed the like of it.* [6:160]

Were you to examine [your state] with fair-mindedness and compassion, you would see that your need for repentance is greater than your need for food, water, and shelter, for sins are veiling you from beholding the Unseen and stand between you and the Beloved. The greatest veils between a servant and his Lord are the veils of sins, for these are made of darkness, whereas other veils, even though the wayfarer should seek to remove them, are made of light and do not imply total remoteness. The likeness of the veil that results from sins is that of a wall that stands between you and the object of your quest, and thus prevents you from seeing any part, trace or shadow of it. On the other hand, veils of light are like glass showing what is behind it to a greater or lesser extent according to how thick or thin it is, but never hiding everything as the wall does - at the very least a shadow must be seen. As it is with physical vision, so it is with the heart. When its eye, which is called 'inner sight' [*baṣīra*], is covered with the darkness of sins, that is, with 'that which covers' [*rayn*], 'that which 'stamps' [*ṭabᶜ*], and 'that which seals' [*khatm*], it sees nothing of the lights of the Unseen and the person is therefore unconcerned with the evil and sins that he commits. When he repents, the veil of sins is removed from the eye of the heart and he perceives that which is God's.[27] He thus becomes fearful of His chastisement and hopeful for His recompense, and then cleaves to acts of obedience and avoids sins. At this stage the veil becomes a veil of light ensuing from his dependence on these acts and his belief that it is he who has caused them to exist. Then God the Exalted removes this veil through the *baraka* of his obedience, and he sees that he is in God's debt for His having led him to these acts and comes to perceive his shortcomings in thanking Him for them. He sees that the Giver and the Withholder is none other than God the Exalted, and that when He wishes good for His servant He bestows on him the garb of *taqwā* to render him worthy of being introduced to His presence. Nothing is in the slave's hand, either for good or ill. Everything is in the hand of God.

When the veil is lifted from the eye of the heart he thinks that he has arrived to God the Exalted, because of the spiritual delight that this station entails. Then, if he is to be enveloped by [God's] hidden solicitude, this veil is also removed. He then passes through veil after veil, as described in this book, until he reaches the Seat of Truth[28] and the places of the beloved ones, so do understand, and do not think that because we have likened the veils to glass that God the Exalted is something to be seen with the physical eye, for He is high above that. May God take charge of your guidance!

Know that repentance is to regret the sins one has committed, for he has said, may God's blessings and peace be upon him: 'Remorse is repentance.' It is also essential to resolve never to repeat them and to avoid previous patterns of behaviour as far as possible. This kind of repentance, which is to feel remorseful about past misdeeds, is the 'repentance of the commonalty' and is always acceptable [to God]. As for the 'repentance of the elect', it is from everything that distracts one from God the Exalted, whereas that of the 'elect of the elect' is from unawareness and distraction in their presence with God the Exalted. This is the repentance of the *ṣiddīqūn,* those intelligent people who have come to recognise the position of their own selves and that each of their breaths is an opportunity worth more than the world and all it contains.

Chapter One

The Inciting Soul: Its wayfaring, world, location, state, wārid, *attributes and evils, and the way to rid oneself of it and ascend beyond it to the second station where the soul becomes Reproachful*

Its wayfaring is 'toward' God.
Its world is the Visible World [*ᶜālam al-shahāda*].
Its location is the chest.
Its state is inclination.
Its *wārid* is *Sharīᶜa*.

This Inciting Soul is the Rational Soul and the heart, of which God the Exalted says, *This is for those possessed of a heart.* [50:37] It is not the piece of flesh that is meant, but the lordly subtle thing [*al-laṭīfa al-Rabbāniyya*]. However, when it becomes impure because of its inclination to its [material] nature, finds rest in its appetites, and consorts with the Appetitive Soul or Vital Spirit, it rejoins the rank of animals and its praiseworthy attributes are changed into blameworthy ones. It then comes to differ from animals only in its outer form, and the Devil becomes one of its troops. Its attributes then include ignorance, avarice, greed, arrogance, irascibility, gluttony, lust, resentful envy, distraction, bad character, delving into that which does not concern it, whether by speech or otherwise, mockery, hatred, injurious behaviour whether with the hand or tongue, as well as the other evil soul, the same one that Zulaykhā spoke of in the course of her story with Yūsuf al-Ṣiddīq,[22] may peace be upon him: *'The soul is indeed an inciter to evil.'* [12:53] And our Prophet Muḥammad, may God's blessings and peace be upon him, said: 'Your worst enemy is your soul which lies between your two flanks', and: 'We have returned from the lesser *jihād* to the greater *jihād.*' This is because it is under the sway of its [material] nature, unable to differentiate between right and wrong, or between good and evil. It is solely through it that the accursed Devil is able to exercise any influence on man. Therefore be wary of it, O my brother, and never trust it. Do not support and aid it when it suffers injury from others; on the contrary, ally yourself with them against it, for when you become convinced of its enmity it becomes necessary for you to do all those things that we have spoken of earlier. It also becomes necessary that you reduce your food, drinking, and sleep, so as to weaken the animal Appetitive Soul, for when it weakens it becomes easier for the higher, nobler and more dignified soul, which is called Reproachful, to free itself of it.

Let your invocation at this stage be *Lā ilāha illa'Llāh*, the meaning of which is that none is to be worshipped by right save God. He says (Exalted is He): *Remember Me and I shall remember you.* [2:152] And the Prophet has said, may God's blessings and peace be upon him, speaking on behalf of his Lord: 'I am as My servant thinks of Me, and I am with him when he remembers Me. When he remembers Me within himself, I remember him within Myself, and when he mentions Me in an assembly, I mention him in a better assembly. When he draws nearer to Me by the span of a hand, I draw nearer to him by the length of an arm, and when he draws nearer to Me by an arm's length, I draw nearer to him by two arms' span, and when he comes to Me walking, I come to him running.' This *ḥadīth*, which is authentic by consensus, indicates the immense merit of remembrance and how small works by the servant are met with great Divine rewards.

The Prophet has also declared, may blessings and peace be upon him: 'Remember God with such frequency that they say "He is mad!".' This *ḥadīth* was narrated by the imām Ibn Ḥibbān[29] in his collection of sound *ḥadīths.*

And he also said, may blessings and peace be upon him: 'The likeness of the one who remembers his Lord and the one who does not is that of the living and the dead.'

And: 'No charity is better than the remembrance of God the Exalted. Were a man to put some money in his lap and proceed to give it away, while another remembered God the Exalted, the one who remembered God the Exalted would be the better of the two.'

And: 'Shall I not inform you of which of your works are best, highest in the sight of your Sovereign, most elevating to your degree, better for you than spending gold and silver, and better for you than to meet your enemies so that you strike at their necks and they strike at yours?' They said: 'Yes, O Messenger of God,' and he said: 'The remembrance of God the Exalted.'

And he said, may blessings and peace be upon him: 'No act is more likely to save a servant from God's chastisement than the remembrance of God the Exalted.' They enquired: 'Not even *jihād* for God?' and he replied: 'Not even *jihād* for God, unless you were to wield your sword until it broke thrice.'

And he said: 'I and the Prophets before me have said nothing superior to *Lā ilāha illa'Llāh*.' And: '*Lā ilāha illa'Llāh* is the best of invocations and the best of deeds. The people who most benefit from my intercession are those who utter it with sincerity. No servant utters it, and then dies still upholding it, but that he shall enter the Garden; even were he to commit adultery and theft, even were he to commit adultery and theft, even were he to commit adultery and theft.'

And he said: 'Renew your faith!' They asked: 'How do we renew our faith, O Messenger of God?' He said: 'Say *Lā ilāha illa'Llāh* in abundance. The uttering of it allows no sin to remain, no other deed resembles it, and no veil comes between it and God until it reaches Him.'

And: 'When you pass by the meadows of the Garden, graze!' They said: 'O Messenger of God, what are the meadows of the Garden?' And he replied: 'The circles of remembrance.'

And: 'No people ever sit together and then separate without having remembered God but that they separate as if they had [just feasted] on the carcass of an ass, and they shall regret it greatly on the Day of Arising.'

And he said, may blessings and peace be upon him: 'The people of the Garden regret nothing save those moments which passed by [in the world] without their remembering God.'

And he said, may blessings and peace be upon him: 'The one who prays the dawn prayer [*ṣalāt al-fajr*] in congregation, sits down remembering God until sunrise, then prays two *rakᶜas*, shall receive a recompense equal to that of a *ḥajj* and an *ᶜumra* that are complete, complete, complete.'

And he said, may blessings and peace be upon him: 'To sit with people who remember God from the dawn prayer till sunrise is more pleasing to me than to free four of the descendants of Ismāᶜīl;[30] and to sit with people who remember God from the afternoon [*ᶜaṣr*] prayer until sunset is more pleasing to me than to free another four.'

And he said, may blessings and peace be upon him: 'To remember God the Exalted in the company of other people after the dawn prayer and until the sun rises is more beloved to me than the world and all it contains.'

And he said, may blessings and peace be upon him: 'To remember God the Exalted in the company of other people after the afternoon prayer and until the sun sets is more beloved to me than the world and all that it contains.'

And he said, may blessings and peace be upon him, speaking on behalf of his Lord, Mighty and Majestic is He: '*Lā ilāha illa'Llāh* is My fortress, and whosoever enters My fortress shall be safe from My torment.'

Care must be taken by those who use this good word as an invocation to prolong the syllable *lā,* clearly accentuate the *i* of *ilāha,* pronounce the *ha* lightly, and cut short the *h* at the end of the Divine Name [so as not to make it a *ha*], and allow no interval between the *ha* and *illa'Llāh.* They should not neglect to articulate the *i* in *ilāha,* otherwise it becomes *ya* and their invocation becomes *layilāha* which is no longer the Word of *Tawḥīd*; there would therefore be neither recompense nor effect to be expected from it. Most invokers fall into this unaware. As he begins to say *Lā ilāha* the invoker must remove from his heart all objects of worship other than God and utter *Lā ilāha* with force and intensity, hurling it at the left side of his chest. He must have presence and awe, keep his eyes closed, and remain ritually pure from all soiling things.

Beware, O invoker, of eating *ḥarām* food. If all vices arise from a stomach filled with *ḥalāl,* how must it be with one filled with *ḥarām*? You must know everything that you need concerning how to purify yourself, make your ablutions, remove impurities, pray and so on. And you must also know something in the way of doctrine, such as knowledge of the Necessary Existent (Transcendent is He!), His Eternal Attributes, that which is necessary, impossible, and possible for Him. You must not occupy yourself with sciences other than these until you have purified your soul and cleansed your heart, for before this you are in dire need of freeing yourself from the prison of your nature and of polishing the mirror of your heart so that the overlying rust that prevents it from perceiving the realities of things is removed. For the heart in this station is covered with the rust of arrogance, greed, resentful envy, conceit, hatred, and the other things that you perceive within yourself, so that your most important duty in this station is to free yourself from those impurities which prevent the heart from reaching the exalted degrees. This is achieved by remembrance with energy and abundance, and by a reduction of food and sleep in order to narrow the devil's paths of entry and to draw the heart nearer to its Lord. For this is the first station, that in which the soul is termed Inciting. It is also called 'nature's prison' and 'the lowest of the low.' Gaining release from it takes priority over everything else. The Shaykhs recommend remembrance aloud to awaken the faculties from their distraction. Therefore, maintain forceful remembrance, keep within the limits of *sharīʿa*, call yourself to account frequently, and instil fear into your soul by reminding it of death, the torments of the grave, the terrors following it, and hell with its torments.

In this station two states alternate: fear and hope. When you are moved from it, your fear changes into Constriction [*qabḍ*] and your hope into Expansion [*basṭ*]. Then when you reach the degrees of perfection, Constriction becomes majesty, and Expansion beauty. Remember, therefore, those things that arouse fear, for it is of more benefit than hope. However, if fear should carry you to the point of despair, then bring to mind the things that arouse hope, such as the immensity of God's mercy, forgiveness and generosity. Humble yourself and surrender to Him. Ask Him to grant you release by His solicitude and graciousness.

Be abundant in your pleas, do not grow weary, and do not say that God the Exalted does not accept from you, for that would cut you off from the Real. The Prophet said, may blessings and peace be upon him: 'Prayer [*duʿāʾ*] *is* worship'; then he recited God's words (Exalted is He!): '*And your Lord said: Call Me and I shall answer you. Those who are too proud to worship Me shall enter hell.*' [40:60–1] To say that 'prayer *is* worship' means that it is the most important part of it, just as [on another occasion he said that] '*Ḥajj* is *ʿArafa*.'[31] Since the supplicant's state is extreme humility and submissiveness to his Lord, being in dire need of Him to grant him his request, and since worship is itself submissiveness and humility, prayer is its most important part on that account. And he also said, may God's blessings and peace be upon him: 'Prayer is the marrow of worship.' The 'marrow' of a thing is its essence. Prayer is the marrow because the supplicant renounces attributing any power or ability whatsoever to himself and acknowledges that everything belongs exclusively to God. The Prophet said, may God's blessings and peace be upon him: 'When the door of prayer is opened for you, the doors of response are opened also.' And: 'Prayer revokes the decrees of destiny, benevolence increases provision, and a bondsman's provision may be withheld because of a sin that he has committed.' For prayer to 'revoke the decrees of destiny' means that it makes them lighter and easier to bear. As for his saying that the bondsman is withheld provision because of a sin, how is this to come about when he has said in another *ḥadīth* that sin does not diminish provision? We can say only that it does at times and not at others, depending on variations in persons and circumstances. He has said, may blessings and peace be upon him: 'The decrees of destiny are revoked only by prayer.' And: 'Prayers are among God's mustered troops, they revoke the decrees after they have been decided.' Their being 'troops' means that they represent the means to reach an end, just as troops are the means to repulse and vanquish the enemy. He also said, may blessings and peace be upon him: 'Caution avails nothing with destiny, and prayers avail for both that which has been decided and that which has not. Hardship comes down and is met by prayers, and they join battle with each other till the Day of Rising.' The definition of 'to battle' in the dictionary is 'to have conflict and war.' And he said, may blessings and peace be upon him: 'Nothing is dearer to God than prayer.' And: 'God becomes wrathful against the one who does not petition Him.' And: 'Weaken not in your prayers, for none perishes who prays.' ('Weaken not' means 'do not abandon prayer, thinking that the answer is too long in coming'.) And: 'The one who wishes God to answer him when in hardship and adversity, let him pray in abundance in his days of affluence,' that is, when possessing wealth and good health. And: 'Prayer is the weapon of the believer, the pillar of religion, and the light of the heavens and earth,' which means that just as a weapon, when sharp-edged and unsheathed, is a means to subdue the enemy, so too does prayer, accompanied by submissiveness, presence of heart, and *ḥalāl* provision, repulse hardships and subdue enemies. Without [these conditions] it resembles a blunt or sheathed sword. And he said, may blessings and peace be upon him: 'No Muslim lifts his face up to God asking for something but that He grants it him,' meaning that either He grants it immediately or keeps it in store for him.

See how honourable man is in the sight of God, and how He allows his prayers to arrest His decided decrees by lightening them and making hardship easier to bear, and to be of avail for those calamities and hardships that have already come to pass and those that have yet to occur; and how his prayers are so honourable in the sight of God that He becomes wrathful with him when he refrains from praying, and how He made praying to Him not only [a form of] worship, but the very essence of it. All these are pure graces, acts of compassion, and honour to mankind. Does it behove you then to remain heedless of your Lord and attend to His enemies, namely the devil and the world and its pleasures? Will you accept to be loathed as they are and pushed away as they are, having known that yours had been the very best of predispositions? Awaken from your heedlessness, which has ruined, abased, and vilified you, and concentrate on Him Whom you cannot do without, before you are led to Him by the chains of trials.

God the Exalted has said: 'O My servant, when you draw nearer to Me by the span of a hand I draw nearer to you by the length of an arm, and when you draw nearer to Me by the length of an arm I draw nearer to you by the span of two arms, and when you come to Me walking I come to you running.' The meaning is this: 'the one who draws nearer to Me with a few acts of obedience, I reward him abundantly; the more his devotion the more the reward, and if his devotions are performed with deliberation, then the reward comes swiftly.' Abandon, therefore, all procrastination, turn away from that which distracts you from your Lord, be content with what you possess, whether it be scarce or plentiful, that it may help you. Abandon ephemeral pleasures to their people. Delay not repentance, nor your approach to God, for you do not know how much of your life still remains. He has said, may blessings and peace be upon him: 'Leave the world to its people. The one who takes more than he needs from the world is unknowingly taking his own ruin.' This means that the one who is engrossed in worldly pursuits which exceed his needs is pursuing his own destruction unaware.

As long as you are in this narrow and vile station you must concentrate on your release from the confines of the ego to the open space of the spirit. Your quest should be to divest yourself of all the blameworthy attributes that we have spoken of earlier and acquire their opposite praiseworthy traits. Substitute, therefore, your pride for humility, your hatred for love, your ostentation for sincerity, your fame for obscurity, until there is no-one left who still either commends or condemns you. Know, also, that when you have purified your self of these faults you will behold certain marvels and mysteries, by the help of God.

Chapter Two

The Reproachful Soul: An exposition of its wayfaring, world, location, state, wārid, *attributes, and the remedies to be used to rid oneself of it and ascend beyond it to the third station; that is, the station in which the soul becomes Inspired*

Its wayfaring is 'for' God.
Its world is the Intermediate Realm [*barzakh*].
Its location is the heart.
Its state is love.
Its *wārid* is *Sharī*ᶜ*a*.

Its attributes are reproachfulness, reflection, conceit, objecting to other people, secret ostentation, and the love of fame and leadership.

There may remain traces of the Inciting Soul in it; yet despite these it is able to acknowledge truth as truth and falsehood as falsehood, and recognise its attributes as blameworthy. Good actions are performed, night vigils, fasts, and so on, but these are contaminated with conceit and secret ostentation. The possessor of such a soul conceals his good actions and acts for God [not for people], yet he loves others to find out about his actions. He loves to be praised and lauded for his acts, yet he detests this tendency, which he recognises in himself, and is unable to erase it entirely from his heart. To erase it entirely would mean that he is sincere and secure; however, even sincere people are still in grave danger, since they like to know that they are sincere and this itself amounts to a secret ostentation. As for open ostentation, it is to act for the sake of being seen by others; this is the 'hidden idolatry' which is wholly to be condemned.

Know that if you possess these attributes you are in the second station and your soul is called Reproachful. It is a station in which one is never safe from perils, even when sincere in one's conduct, as explained above. It is the second station in the journey of the Ones Brought Near,[32] the seekers of extinction [*fanā'*] from themselves and subsistance [*baqā'*] by their Lord. They are commanded to die before their time, their master having bidden them: 'Die before you die!' They thus strive to die the death of the self. As for the Righteous [*abrār*], who are the Companions of the Right Hand, it is their ultimate dwelling and their highest station. This is why it was said that 'The good acts of the Righteous are the bad acts of the Ones Brought Near,' for the latter do not halt at this second station, but ascend from one station to another until they reach the seventh. There are thus five more stations after this one, the circumstances of which we shall discuss in detail in the following chapters. The Ones Brought Near do not stop at this station because of the great dangers and constant fatigue that it involves; for its highest degree is sincerity, and the sincere are in peril, salvation from this peril being only by extinction to the sight of one's sincerity by the contemplative witnessing [*shuhūd*] that none causes movement or stillness but God the Exalted.

This contemplation depends on travelling the path of the Ones Brought Near, for the Righteous do not perceive even the fragrance of it. By both proof and unveiling the Ones Brought Near acquire the certainty that God the Exalted has prescribed the acts of worship to make them doorways through which those whom He wishes enter His Presence. They thus pass through them to Him, in order to submit themselves before Him and gaze at Him with their inner eyes. Yet they neither accord those [acts] much consideration nor depend on them, nor admire them, but see that it was by His grace that God unlocked the doors of these acts of worship for them, allowed them to enter, and made them worthy of being accepted [by Him]. People in such a state are in no need of sincerity. It does not even cross their minds, for they perceive none of their works as their own, and thus they perceive no act to be other than God's and thus liable to be complained about. As opposed to this, the Righteous never reach this contemplative vision; they perceive themselves as having created their actions and are therefore required to show sincerity in them. Because they do not see that God the Exalted is the creator of all acts they are therefore likely to complain about some of them and hence become subject to toil and weariness. They thus become such that, even were they to enter a lizard's hole, God would cause something or other in it to injure them. This is because of the human nature in them which causes conceit, arrogance, rancour, envy, bad character, hatred, enmity, being engrossed in earning a livelihood, and other such things. These inevitably yield trouble, weariness, and a constriction of the breast.

An example must be provided to explain the difference between the Righteous and the Ones Brought Near, and the toiling of the first and the repose of the second. The example is that of a great evil tree that has many branches, each of which produces one kind of lethal poison. A group of people arrive and proceed to cut the branches, leaving the trunk, together with its water supply, intact. They neither cut the trunk nor its water supply that it might dry out and they might thus be rid of it. They are therefore unable to be entirely rid of the poisons, for whenever they cut a branch another quickly grows, since the trunk remains. Another group arrives and proceeds to sever the tree's water supply. The branches will now grow weaker and cease to produce poison, and those people will be rid of them and relieved of the need to cut them repeatedly, for they would prove impossible to get rid of entirely since whenever some are cut others grow in their place. This tree represents man's stomach, and the branches the blameworthy attributes which we have mentioned. The produce of the tree represents the outward consequences of these attributes. The Righteous, having learned by way of proof that these attributes are ruinous, both in this world and the next, strive to remove them gradually but are unable to be entirely rid of any of them. When they are free of one on one day it reappears the next, and thus they remain until they die. This is because filling their stomach renders their nature stronger and their blood more abundant, so that the Devil becomes more able to take hold of them. The Prophet, may blessings and peace be upon him, said: 'The son of Adam fills no vessel worse than his stomach,' and 'The devil runs within you with the blood, therefore straiten his paths with hunger.' There is no doubt that those whom the devil takes hold of and runs in their veins as blood does must exhibit blameworthy attributes and be unable to complete the removal of any of them, even though they may be removed temporarily as a consequence of the fear aroused by hearing of the horrors of the grave, the two angels, hell and its keepers, and the Resurrection. Whenever the fear subsides, however, the attributes reappear.

As for the Ones Brought Near, they learn both by way of proof and by experience that the stomach is at the origin of corruption and blameworthy attributes, and therefore strive to reduce its evil effects by reducing their food intake. They are then able to rid themselves of all blameworthy attributes and acquire praiseworthy ones. This is because when they eat less they drink less, sleep less, and speak less. The hungry man who keeps vigil at night is disinclined to speak. They isolate themselves from the people, and of the blameworthy attributes no trace survives in their hearts.

If you have understood this example you will have grasped the difference between the Righteous and the Ones Brought Near. You should know that the Righteous are acceptable to God; they are people of *taqwā,* but yet they are unable to rid themselves of all blemishes and are therefore unable to be entirely free of trouble, both in this world and the next. However, God has promised that He will recompense them in the hereafter. As for the Ones Brought Near, they are the few who are immersed in the contemplation of the Real, so much so that they forget creation and never think of the pleasures of this world, nor of the delights of the next. Whence, then, can harm befall them?

The saying of the Prophet, may God's blessings and peace be upon him: 'Were a believer to enter a lizard's hole, God would cause something there to harm him,' and similar *ḥadīths* are taken to refer to the Righteous; and you are now aware of their state.

Know that if you occupy yourself constantly with the Name with which your shaykh has inculcated you, the path will be shortened for you; on the other hand if you delay and neglect it the path will be lengthened, so blame yourself alone. *Jihād* is an obligation, and the essence of it is to forsake all habits. Habits are many, but the shaykhs have determined those pillars of the path that cannot be done without. These are six: To eat, sleep and talk less; to isolate oneself from people; to make remembrance constantly and to reflect effectively. Moderation is required in each of these things; hence they have said that food and the other things are only to be diminished, not abandoned altogether. The effective thing in this path is to eat only when hungry, and then to less than satiety. The Prophet, may God's blessings and peace be upon him, omitted supper when he had eaten lunch, and omitted lunch when he had eaten supper.

Occupy yourself in this station with the second Name, that is, *Allāh*. It indicates that Essence the existence of which is necessary and deserving of all praise. Cut short the end letter of this and all other Names, in this instance the *h*. This is what authorities on this matter have stated. Use this Name in abundance, for only with abundance will you profit and will wonders appear. Do this while standing, sitting, and lying down, night and day.[33] Assign to yourself times when you will sit facing the *qibla,* shut your eyes, and utter this invocation which is the Greatest Name. Utter it forcefully and loudly, raise your face up then bring it down on your chest, turning neither right nor left, contrary to what you had been doing when invoking the first Name, that is turning from right to left. Emphasise the *A* in *Allāh,* cut the *h* short, prolong the *ā* that precedes it. Beware of being in such a hurry as to say *Allāhalāhalā*. This will happen only if you do not emphasise the *A*, but if you do, it will not.

Know that in this station you will be full of thoughts and of whisperings, especially when your invocation is uttered midway between being unheard and being loud. However, when you invoke loudly the thoughts will diminish. This Name is a fire with which you burn all thoughts and whisperings. The path of the People [*al-qawm*] is ardour and effort. Those who earnestly expend their effort obtain everything that they desire, while those who delay and neglect are obstructed on the road. There are numerous obstructions, the greatest of which is to depend on created beings, feel inclined toward them, and keep their intimate company. How can one hope to arrive who mixes with them and keeps their company in the manner that they do with each other, that is, talking, joking, laughing and so on? If you desire the exalted stations, abandon creation and concentrate on your Lord. Feel estranged from all people, until they say about you that you are mad;[34] only then will you see wonders, God willing. But if you do not conform with what has just been said, your times will pass in trouble and toil and you will reach nothing of what you desire. Be earnest and strive, do not content yourself with trivia and mere verbosity, test yourself, do not be credulous with your soul, tell your shaykh about the evil in it and hide nothing from him. Be sincere in your quest, and your effort and the wonders and secrets of the heart will become unveiled for you. You will enter the World of Similitudes [*ʿālam al-mithāl*], which is a world other than the one you are now in. It is the first station of the Ones Brought Near, and there the wayfarer beholds that which the five senses cannot grasp. It is a state that is intermediate between sleep and wakefulness, and it usually comes to the wayfarer as he is sitting down, and then he sees what he sees. Its condition is that he be aware of the time and place and of his state between sleep and wakefulness, for if he is not it is only a dream and thus to be discounted in this regard.

Know that God has made it the rule that progression from

the second to the third station occurs only at the hand of a gnostic [*ʿārif*] guide who knows the path's waystations and conditions. The same thing applies to progression from the third to the fourth station, except that then the help of a perfect guide is required, not only that of a knowledgeable one. The perfect guide is more than a gnostic. As for promotion from the fourth station to the fifth, sixth, and seventh, it does not usually require a guide.[35] God it is Who grants success.

Chapter Three

The Inspired Soul: Its wayfaring, world, location, state, wārid, *attributes, and the remedy wherewith to traverse it and rise to the fourth Station where the soul is called Serene*

Its wayfaring is 'upon' God, which means that in this station the wayfarer's sight falls only upon God the Exalted, since the reality of faith has permeated him inwardly, and everything other than God the Exalted has become extinct in his contemplative vision.

Its world is the World of Spirits.

Its location is the spirit.

Its state is passionate love.

Its *wārid* is gnosis [*maʿrifa*].

Its attributes are: liberality, resignation, knowledge, forgiving people, inviting them to rectitude, accepting their excuses, and seeing that God the Exalted is holding everything that walks the earth by the forelock.[36] No possible objection to any created being thus remains. Among its attributes also are yearning, transports, weeping, restlessness, shunning creation and attending to the Real, changefulness [*talwīn*], a succession of constriction [*qabḍ*] and expansion [*basṭ*], the absence of fear and hope, pleasure in agreeble singing, being transported with delight on listening to it, the love of *dhikr*, affability, joy with God, uttering words of wisdom and knowledge, and contemplative vision. These and similar attributes are those of the Inspired Soul, which is thus called because the Real (Exalted is He!) inspires it with both corruption and righteousness,[37] and it has come to hear, without intermediary, the whisperings of the angel and those of the devil, whereas in the previous station it heard nothing, being still close to the degree of animals. Because of this hearing of the whisperings of the angel and the devil, this station is difficult and the wayfarer needs a guide to take him away from the obscurities of doubts to the light of theophanies [*tajalliyyāt*].

In this station the wayfarer's state is weak and he is unable to differentiate between Majesty and Beauty, nor can he differentiate between what the angel suggests to him and what the devil insinuates, for he is not altogether free of his [lower] nature and the entailments of his human state. He is in danger, if ever he forgets himself, of plummeting down to the *Lowest of the Low*,[38] that is, back to the first station, that in which the soul is called Inciting. He would then return to his previous pattern of eating too much, drinking too much, sleeping too much, and carelessly mixing with people; and his beliefs might suffer corruption. He may then abandon his acts of devotion, commit sins and then pretend that he is a man of *tawḥīd* to whom things have been unveiled and who has become an authority on contemplation, and may claim that others who strive in obedience are veiled from this contemplation. Once his belief becomes corrupted he perishes along with the rest of those who are to perish. The fire of his [lower nature] is released upon his heart and burns whatever faith it contains. His effort and toil have been wasted and he attains none of his desires; on the contrary, he becomes a devil, himself astray and leading others astray. He catches glimpses of devilish imaginations and takes them for Divine manifestations. This happens after his human nature has weakened and his spirituality has become stronger, and the deafness of his heart has gone and its release drawn nearer, when only a little remains for him to enter the presence of the August King, when the forerunners of *tawḥīd* are beginning to appear and he has become stronger in self-discipline, effort, and divestment.

The reason why this catastrophe befalls this wayfarer as he

approaches the station of perfection is that he is still not remote from the first station, that where the soul is termed Inciting; and when because of his self-discipline [*mujāhada*] some of the veils are stripped away, the fear that had been caused by their presence also disappears. This fear used to hold him back from sins and drive him to more devotions. Few are those who, when their fear subsides, maintain their scrupulous adherence to *sharīʿa*. You are therefore urged, in this station, to follow your shaykh, even if your ego insinuates to you that you are nearer [to God] than he is. You must adhere to *sharīʿa*, conform to the rules of courtesy, force yourself to perform your *awrād*, and restrain your soul with the fetters of *ṭarīqa*, even though it might find this difficult. In this station the soul is inclined to freedom and carelessness, and the required thing is to oppose it until it comes to rest by reaching the fourth station, where it will be called Serene.

This Serene station means happiness in the two abodes,[39] and whenever a wayfarer sets his foot therein he is saved by God's help from all the diseases of the soul, since he has ascended to the first degree of perfection. So rise, O seeker of perfection! Abandon the soul's trivia, do not be deceived by whatever *tawḥīd* has appeared to you, and do not make it the cause of your rout or obstruction in your quest. On the contrary, make use of it in tearing whatever veils of lights still remain. Do not be distracted by those flashes from the higher worlds that you perceive as you travel along your path, for these are veils that will prevent you from approaching the Highest Essence and may be the cause of your return to the level of the animals. Keep to the things that have led you to reach your state of unveiling and you will be safe from danger. This means continuing to keep night vigils, fasts, isolation from mankind, and silence, and holding firmly to your shaykh, if he is one who is perfect. Inform him of the thoughts that occur to you, whether they be good or evil. The more you believe in your shaykh the more you will drawn be to the World of Sanctity [*ʿālam al-quds*], and the weaker will be the pull of your human nature.

It may happen to you, in this station, that you begin to think that you are more knowledgeable than your shaykh. This notion would cut you off from the flow of his spiritual assistance [*madad*]. Therefore expel this thought by reading about the attributes of the perfect ones, and, when you come to recognise him as perfect, enter into his fold with the conviction that your deliverance is in his hands. Endure whatever harm may come to you from him.[40] Be with him as a corpse in the hands of the washer, who moves it as he wills. Beware of being critical of any of his states, and, if you perceive any objections within yourself, inform him and repent before him. It may happen that you see him in a situation that deserves criticism. You may see him, for instance, reproaching his servant for wasting something of no value, or showing annoyance at the loss of that thing. Counteract your criticism with the thought that the states of the Perfect are not to be measured by the same yardstick as those of others, and none but God the Exalted knows the inner reality of the Perfect.

If you are unable to find a perfect shaykh, heal yourself by conforming to *sharīʿa*, keeping to regular invocations such as have been handed down from the Prophet, may God's blessings and peace be upon him, asking for forgiveness in abundance, and keeping the company of the righteous. These things apply when you are in danger and the evil in your soul is overpowering the good. On the other hand, if you are not in danger, and the good in your soul has overpowered the evil, then feel delighted and transported, throw off constraint, shun all turbidity, do not be preoccupied with either paradise or hell, and pay no attention to those who criticise you for throwing off constraint, even at the cost of their being angry with you and shunning you. So different is the object of your quest from the object of theirs that no harmony between you is possible, for their aim is lowly and yours exalted, and these are opposites which cannot unite. *So turn away from those who shun the remembrance of Us and want nothing but the life of this world.* [53:29]

The gist of all this is that this third Station is one that contains both good and evil, so that if the good in the soul overcomes the evil it is raised to the high stations, but if the evil overcomes the good it is abased to the lowest level, so that the wayfarer must then again exhaust and humble his soul in the manner described earlier. The sign that the good is overcoming the evil is that you see yourself inwardly alive with the reality of faith [*īmān*], and outwardly alive with the *sharīʿa* of Islam. This is to have the inner certainty that everything in existence moves according to the Divine will and by the Divine ability, and yet to remain outwardly active in obedience and far removed from all major sins and most minor ones, whether when amongst people or in solitude.

This is the sign that the good is overcoming the evil. As for the evil overcoming the good, the sign of this is that the wayfarer's experience of the reality of faith increases, but much of his human nature remains. He does not conform outwardly with *sharīʿa,* he abandons devotions and may, unsurprisingly, commit sins. This is because when his perception of reality grows stronger and he sees that his acts are according to the Divine will, he becomes veiled by the lights of *ḥaqīqa* from the secrets of *sharīʿa*. He is consequently driven from the doorway of the Divine Presence, he halts with the flashes [*lawā'iḥ*] that suit his disposition, and loses both his world and his religion. The evil in him overcomes the good and he becomes a *zindīq* who adheres to no religion.

Know that God's satisfaction and His theophanies [*tajalliyyāt*] reach His slave solely through the door of obedience, while His wrath, banishment, and remoteness befall the servant solely through the door of sins. So stand humbly at the doors of *sharīʿa* and ask your Lord for everything that you need, for he shall respond and you will not be turned away disappointed. Beware of being deceived by whatever may appear to you in this station that will bring with it banishment and cursing; you would thus be following your caprice and straying from the path of God. May He take charge of your guidance!

Help yourself to achieve your desires in this station by reciting the third Name, which is *Hū!* Let it be accompanied at first with the vocative *Yā,* then [recite it] without it. Let this be at all times, while standing, sitting, or lying down, by night and by day, so that by its *baraka* you may escape the danger of this station. It also severs any attachment the soul may still harbour to the first and second stations, for one's nature is more powerful than any acquired attributes. Hence the soul awaits your moment of inattention, when you relent from pressing and rebuking it, and it immediately resumes its previous pattern.

In this station, exercising pressure on the soul is by passionate love, transports of delight, yearning for reunion and rejoining the beloved, remembering the meetings with the beloved, and enjoying the beauty of the face of the beloved. These strengthen the wayfarer's heart in his earnest progress, and, whenever he feels that he is retreating, his heart breaks and he weeps more and more.

Know, O *ᶜārif* [gnostic], that in this station you are a subtle spiritual being upon whom the sun of contemplation is dawning, towards whom the glad tidings of perfection are approaching, and upon whom the breeze of reunion is blowing. Most of the veils have been lifted from your heart, especially the thickest ones, and your greatest and most evil desires have disappeared. For this is the station of the spirit, and the spirit is still veiled from contemplating the beauty of the Real, and still harbours desires that prevent arrival to His Presence. However, these are veils of light and desires that are acceptable, since they are the desire to see the Real and attain contemplation and reunion. They are due to overpowering yearning which leads to demanding the thing before its time; and this is the condition of all passionate lovers. In this station you are a passionate lover, delighting in humility and neediness, unable to bear separation from your beloved. Throw off constraint, care nothing for scandal, but beware of slipping into thinking that throwing off constraint means abandoning the injunctions of *sharīᶜa*, as those who stray and lead others astray may think, those deviants and heretics who still live in the world of [physical] nature and have no knowledge of *ḥaqīqa* and do not adhere to *sharīᶜa*. They abandon the ritual prayers and fasts, pursue their appetites, and commit sins, while they pretend to be people of *tawḥīd* and lovers of the Divine Presence. As for throwing off constraint in the legally sanctioned manner, its purpose is to remove some of the barriers which obstruct you from reaching your Beloved. These barriers are quite numerous and can be removed only by throwing off constraint in the manner sanctioned by the *sharīʿa*. Sumptuous clothes, for example, are one such barrier. Those afflicted with this habit occupy themselves with the [worldly] stratagems and efforts necessary to be able to afford such clothes and this bars them from their Beloved. If they throw off constraint and wear whatever is to hand and easily obtainable, and concentrate instead on their Beloved, this will be one of the benefits of this condition. Other matters are to be thought of in the same light.

When you do this and the ego which is obstructing you dies, and the *rūḥānīs* address you with injunctions and prohibitions, pay no heed to them. Allow their address to you to cause you neither joy nor sorrow, and concentrate on your Beloved alone. It is better for you to hear nothing, since hearing such things may stop you in your journey, for these are strange matters such as you have never heard before, and you may think that you have reached the end of your quest; your determination may then flag so that you revert to your [lower] nature. This is one of the hazards of this station, so beware of it. Ask your Lord (Transcendent is He!) to assist you in overcoming whatever may obstruct your path to Him, for it is only by Him that you can reach Him.

In this station you will also experience the state of Extinction [*fanā'*] which will assist you to ascend from it to the fourth station, which is where the soul becomes Serene. Extinction in this station is a condition that comes upon the wayfarer and renders him unaware of all sensory things. This is the unawareness of absorption, not that of fainting or sleep. In it one's sensory perception of the environment is affected so that the eye, for instance, becomes unaware of what it sees despite seeing it. The state of the wayfarer becomes as that of a man who has suffered a loss and who, as he walks past a friend, looks him in the face but does not greet him. When asked: 'Why do you pass me by without greeting me?' he answers: 'By God, I did not even see you, so grievous is my loss!' Similarly, the ear does hear sounds, but it is as though it does not. And so it is for the other senses. The mind also becomes unaware of its own contents. This state can be truly known only by those who actually pass through it. This is the first extinction; the second occurs to the wayfarer in the fifth station, where the soul is called Contented, and the third is the disappearance of all his human attributes in the Unitary degree. That which becomes extinct is the slave's attributes, not his very existence, for his existence does not become absorbed in God's, as some ignorant people may think who utter falsehoods concerning God. But when the slave approaches God in servitude and divests himself of the reprehensible attributes which oppose that servitude, then God bestows upon him, through His grace, the praiseworthy attributes to replace them. The Able One is God, and the powerless one is the slave.

Know that during the first extinction you come to hear the speech of the *rūḥānīs,* but not through your sense of hearing – and you are able to understand none of it. When the state of extinction subsides, the understanding then comes to you of what had been said and what had been inspired in you, and you are then able to see what they inscribed in the mirror of your heart. Thereafter, whenever you speak, you shall utter words of wisdom.

O God! O You who give when asked! Deprive us not, and all lovers, of this extinction! Let not our share of it be deprivation; let not this world be our main preoccupation, nor the limit of our knowledge! Drive from us everything that will obstruct us from reaching You, by the honour of the one whom You honour, may Your blessings and peace be upon him!

There are six 'causes' of extinction: remembrance [*dhikr*], reflection [*fikr*], hunger, night vigils, silence, and seclusion. The most important of these is hunger. Therefore, O seeker of extinction, abandon not in this station self-discipline and effort, even when you find them difficult, and forget not their previous benefits. Do not be deceived by whatever gleams [*bāriqāt*] may appear to you without your being able to identify them as either satanic or divine, for you know that it is in this third station that confusion occurs, when the wayfarer is unable to distinguish between the inspiration which comes from the angel and that which comes from Iblīs. When al-Junayd[41] was asked: 'Now that you have reached God, why do you use prayer-beads?' he replied: 'I will not abandon that which brought me to the object of my quest.' So do not be deceived, O wayfarer, by what may appear to you, lest you abandon those things which you have known by experience to be pure and good and which allow you, with God's assistance, to reach the difficult parts of the path. For the ego is an enemy and you should not trust it, even when you have attained the exalted ranks. Persevere in self-discipline and effort, and your love will increase and you will enjoy your state of yearning, intoxication, and the throwing-off of constraint. The station of passionate love is a station of such delight that, because of the intensity of that delight, the lover is reluctant to ascend to a higher station, even though it forms a veil between him and the Beloved. He does not wish to escape the sorrow, distress, grief, and other things that are caused by passionate love; on the contrary, he wishes that state to endure. The state of passionate love is a state that is acceptable to lovers, although compared with those that are higher it may be disparaged. So when he remembers those days the Perfect Man regrets them for the throwing-off of constraint and carelessness which they entailed. But with self-discipline and effort it is a true state, and its possessor is truthful in whatever love poetry he produces. In the absence of self-discipline and effort, by contrast, it is untrue and its possessor is a liar, his poetry is tasteless, has no effect on the hearts of others, and is repulsive to the ear.

In this station, which is that of the spirit (the spirit being the abode of passionate love with its transports and intoxication), the wayfarer stays for a long time; for the lover is oblivious to himself and even to his Beloved, so busy is he with uttering His

Name and with the delight of praising His Beauty in his poems. This happens when the state is one of Expansion [*basṭ*]; but when it is one of Constriction [*qabḍ*] after expansion, and he awakens from the slumber of passionate love, his chest becomes tight and his heart severely aggrieved, and he thus becomes humble and quiet. These two states alternate in the wayfarer until he ascends to the fourth station where he acquires firmness in love; constriction and expansion are then transformed into awe [*hayba*] and intimacy [*uns*]. These latter two are states which alternate in the perfected man and are only to be known by experience. The difference between awe and Constriction is that one becomes impatient with the second but not with the first, and the difference between intimacy and Expansion is that the second is overpowering and may lead to a lack of courtesy with the Real (Transcendent is He!), but not so the first.

To sum up: fear and hope, constriction and expansion, awe and intimacy, and Majesty and Beauty, are no more than two states the names of which change with changes in persons and stations. When they happen to someone whose soul is still Inciting or Reproachful they are called 'fear' and 'hope'. When they befall someone whose soul is Inspired, they are called 'constriction' and 'expansion'. When they occur to someone whose soul is Serene, Contented, or Found Pleasing, they are called 'awe' and 'intimacy'. And when they happen to someone whose soul is Perfect, they are called 'Majesty' and 'Beauty'. Hence fear and hope are for the beginner, constriction and expansion are for the intermediate, awe and intimacy for the perfect, and Majesty and Beauty for the vicegerent [*khalīfa*].

Know that the lordly secrets are hidden in destitution and servitude. Take, therefore, the path of humility and abasement, and you will become one of the 'free slaves'. You will attain none of your desires save through servitude. You may attain some without servitude, but whatever you attain in this manner will never be complete. Ibn ʿAṭa'illāh says in his *Ḥikam*:[42] 'Plant your existence in the soil of obscurity, for the fruit of that which grows from what has not been planted is never complete.' Another Sufi once said: 'Our path suits only those whose egos have been used for wiping rubbish dumps.' And Bishr ibn al-Ḥārith[43] said: 'I know of no man who wished to become known who has not lost his religion and become exposed.' So bury your existence and bide your time until the following sayings of the Prophet become true for you: 'Die before you die,' and 'Whoso wishes to behold a dead man walking the earth let him look at Abū Bakr al-Ṣiddīq.'[19] This death will take the place of natural death in your case, so that when the angel charged with taking your spirit arrives to take you from one abode to another he will greet you with a *salām* and handle you gently, since you have already experienced the voluntary death referred to in the words 'Die before you die.' This is the extinction of which we spoke earlier in this chapter, and which is a state where no inclination remains in the wayfarer for either wealth, children, or any other thing, and where he stands in fear of no kind of harmful thing whatsoever. This is undoubtedly the state of the dead. Furthermore, just as the Intermediary Realm is unveiled for the dead to behold, so is the World of Similitudes [*ᶜālam al-mithāl*], and both are part of the *Malakūt*. What the wayfarer sees when he enters the World of Similitudes varies according to his aptitude and disposition.

If you are one who has reached none of these states, then you should desire them passionately and strive to attain them, for whoso seeks something with sincerity and determination will attain it, by the power of God. Therefore use the kind of self-discipline and effort that we have mentioned, and constantly recite the third Name, for the Names possess undeniable properties which become manifest only when invocation is repeated with abundance and courtesy maintained. This means that the invoker should face the *qibla* whenever possible, sit on his knees or stand, keep his mind free, listen to the invocation attentively, have inward and outward purity, and maintain ritual purity [*wuḍū'*]. If, while maintaining courtesy in this manner, you are also upholding *sharīᶜa*, then your state is sound. Do not be impatient and restless if the Opening is not forthcoming, for it must arrive, even if after a delay. The condition for this is rectitude [*istiqāma*] and the upholding of *sharīʿa*. Use this invocation some of the time: *Lā Hū illā Hū*. This is a formidable invocation. Say it as though you were addressing your bodily parts, telling them that there is nothing in existence but the Real. This is the contemplative vision of the perfected. May God grant us to join them, by the honour of His beloved one, may blessings and peace be upon him!

Chapter Four

The Serene Soul: Its wayfaring, world, location, state, wārid, *attributes, and how to ascend from it to the fifth Station*

Its wayfaring is 'with' God.

Its world is the Muḥammadan Reality [*al-Ḥaqīqa al-Muḥammadiyya*].

Its location is the secret, which is the inner aspect of the spirit, so that when it descends one degree it becomes the 'spirit', and when it descends another it is called the 'heart'.

Its state is sincere serenity.

Its *wārid* is some of the secrets of *sharīʿa.*

Its attributes are: liberality, reliance, forbearance, activity in worship, gratitude, contentment with destiny, and fortitude during hardship.

There are signs to indicate that the wayfarer has reached this station. Among them are that he does not deviate at all from legal injunctions, takes pleasure only in the behaviour pattern of the Chosen One, may God's blessings and peace be upon him, and finds serenity only in following his sayings. This is the station of mastery [*tamkīn*], of the Eye of Certainty, and of perfect faith, whereas the previous station was that of changefulness [*talwīn*].

In this station, the wayfarer is a delight to the eyes of the onlookers and to the ears of his audience. Were he to speak without cease, his words would never be boring or wearisome, since his tongue expresses that which God casts into his heart of the realities of things and the secrets of *sharīʿa*, and he never speaks a word but that it conforms to the words of God and His Messenger. This is why, in this station, the wayfarer must sit with the people some of the time, to give them some of God's favours that are bestowed upon him, and to articulate the wisdom contained in his heart. However, you must have time [alone] with God, because, in this station, you are at the first degree of perfection and should therefore not keep the company of people at all times. This would deprive you of ascending to the remaining stations, that is, the fifth, sixth, and seventh.

In this station, occupy yourself with the fourth Name, which is *Ḥaqq* [Real], both using the vocative *Yā* and without. Do not concern yourself with what may appear to you, and ask your Lord not to show you anything that is likely to distract you from His service and from standing at His doorstep. You will thus see that those among the men of perfection who are 'guarded' when God causes supernatural events [*karāmāt*] to appear through them, are unaware of them and do not know whether or not something extraordinary has happened. It has been related that one of them once walked by a man who threw a pebble at him which struck his heel. He felt nothing, but the man who had thrown the pebble fell down dead. The saint was asked: 'Where is your forgiveness and magnanimity? Is it permissible to slay a soul that God has declared sacrosanct?' He answered: 'By God! I have no knowledge of what you are speaking of, and I do not know the man. However, it is God's wont to honour His friendss, even without their knowing it.'[44] Similar stories abound. Understand, therefore, the intention, and ask God to help you tear down your remaining veils, for the veil in this station is to love and desire supernatural events [*karāmāt*]. So halt not with these, for they are but created things and hold no benefit for you, whether in this world or the next. Know, however, that a *karāma* in itself is not a bad thing, since it is an honour from God the Exalted bestowed upon His servant. It is to love and desire it that is bad.

In this station, your soul desires litanies, invocations [*awrād*], and prayers, and loves the Chosen One, may God's blessings and peace be upon him, with a love that is different from that experienced prior to this station.

Do not trust your soul in any station, for the human creature remains prey to trials and afflictions throughout his life. You must therefore guard yourself against its defects until the day you die.

In this station, you may experience a wish for money to assist you in serving God and helping your brothers. There is no harm in this, but on certain conditions. The first is for your intention to be what we have just mentioned. The second is that your heart should not become so preoccupied with earning that it severs you from your Lord. The third is that when some money comes to you you should not conceal it and appear to be poor.

You may also experience, in this station, the desire for leadership, fame, guiding others, and for being a shaykh, in order to gather the people so that they may be guided at your hands and that you may be recompensed by God. Beware of this, for it is a trick of the ego. However, if it is God who thus establishes you in this station, causes you to become known, and clothes you in the garb of a shaykh without any effort on your part, no desire, and no pursuit, then carry out God's will, for it shall then be better for you than isolation. The sign of this is that your brothers love and obey you, while you do not perceive yourself as better than they, but perceive them as better than you, and you are indebted to them for their belief that they are lower and for their respect for you. If this is how it is between you, then guide them gently, respect them, teach them to love the path, be humble with them, and thank God who has made you qualify for this position of which you are unworthy. Always feel indebted to them, and if you ever think that they are in your debt, then know that you are not one of the knights of this field; abandon this position, leave them, and strive to free your own soul from its remaining blemishes, for this is more important for both you and them.

Some souls are soft and gentle, noble and intelligent by natural disposition. When they cross the stations, they do so smoothly, and when they reach the fourth they deserve to become guides, for they are gentle, affable, and forbearing by nature, and, while crossing the stations, they purify themselves of human turbidities. For them there is no harm in guiding their brothers and prescribing for them the beneficial remedies of this path, on the abovementioned conditions. This applies in the absence of a more perfected guide; but in his presence, one should see him as a Divine gift that allows one to rest and to leave toiling to someone else. Other souls are base and vile. When they cross the stations, and their blameworthy attributes are exchanged for praiseworthy ones, and they reach the fourth station and become Serene, they still do not qualify as guides, since they lack the necessary conditions. They should be in no hurry for this and should complete their ascent to the fifth, sixth, then seventh stations.

Now that you are aware of the differences between souls, you should know that there is no essential difference between those who, like the Khalwatīs, say that the stations the wayfarer ascends through are seven, and those who say that they are three. The non-Khalwatīs do not count the first station, where the soul is called Inciting, but begin with the second, where it is called Reproachful, then the third, where it is called Inspired, then the fourth, where it is called Serene. They do not count the fifth, sixth and seventh, since they consider only the naturally pure souls, which, when they reach the fourth station, are undoubtedly perfect and worthy of guiding others. As for the Khalwatīs, they count them as seven, making the first the Inciting and the last the Perfect Soul. Know that non-Khalwatīs teach the wayfarer three Names only. When his soul is Reproaching, they inculcate him with *Lā ilāha illa'Llāh,* then at the beginning of the Inspired, with *Allāh! Allāh!*, and near its end *Hū! Hū!* With this Name he enters the Serene and they teach him no other Names.

Know that when you complete the fourth station and your soul becomes Serene with the serenity of the All-Merciful, and you depart not one inch from following the Book and *sunna,* and your blood and flesh are permeated with following the *sharīʿa,* then the Hand of [Divine] Mercy gives you the pull of perfection, which is not the same as the first pull at the beginning of the journey. Then you become forgetful of the things of this world and the next, unless they be present before you; and when they are absent they also become absent from your mind. This is because your heart is continuously contemplating the Beauty and Majesty of the Real.

Chapter Five

The Contented Soul: Its wayfaring, world, location, state, wārid, *attributes, and how to ascend from it to the sixth Station*

Its wayfaring is 'in' God.

Its world is the *Lāhūt.*

Its location is the Secret of the Secret, which is that which is known only to the Real.

Its state is Extinction [*fanā'*], but not in the manner explained earlier, which is the senses' unawareness of the objects of perception, for that state was that of those in the middle of the path, whereas here it is that of people who are nearing the end of their journey and approaching the state of Subsistence [*baqā'*]. 'Extinction' here signifies the elimination of human attributes until Subsistence is reached, but not immediately. The Extinction that is then followed by immediate Subsistence is the Truth of Certainty [*ḥaqq al-yaqīn*]. It occurs after the one which is spoken of here, that is, in the seventh station.

The Contented Soul has no *wārid,* for the *wārid* comes only when attributes still remain, and in this station they are no longer there, not even traces of them. This is why, in this station, the wayfarer is extinct, neither subsistent by himself as he had been before, nor subsistent by God as he will be in the seventh station. This is a state that can be discerned only experientially. However, a perfect guide may be able to explain it to a seeker who has himself reached [a degree of] perfection.

The attributes of this soul are: detachment from everything other than God the Exalted, sincerity, scrupulousness, and a contented acceptance of everything that occurs in the universe, without so much as a quiver of the heart, without resorting to spiritual concentration to fend off an injury, and without objecting to anything at all. This is because the soul is absorbed in the contemplation of absolute Beauty. This state does not prevent the wayfarer from guiding and counselling people, and no-one hears his words without benefiting from them. All this occurs while his heart is occupied with the World of Divinity [*Lāhūt*] and the Secret of the Secret.

The man in this station is immersed in the ocean of courtesy with God the Exalted. His prayers are never turned down; however, out of modesty and courtesy, he never allows his tongue to utter a request unless forced to do so. When forced, he asks and his prayer is never refused.

He is honourable in the sight of created beings, respected by all men, great and small, for he has received the address of the Presence of Nearness: 'Today you are established firmly in Our favour and in Our trust.'[45] Created beings are obliged to respect him, but he does not rely on them, especially if he is poor and they treat him well, for souls are naturally inclined to love those who treat them well. So occupy yourself with your Lord, for if you do so their longing for you will increase, and if you do deserve a share of what they possess it will come to you without action on their part. Do not rely on them, neither harbour any wish for what they possess. Do not shun them because of their eagerness for you. When they come to you with love do not flee them. Rely on your Lord.

In this station, occupy yourself with the fifth Name, which is *Ḥayy* [Alive]. It means the One who possesses life and over whom death holds no sway. Repeat it abundantly so that your extinction may depart and be replaced by subsistence by the Alive, and you then enter the sixth station and are promoted from standing at the doorstep to the places of the Beloved.

Know that there are Names that are called 'Subsidiary Names', and these are: *al-Wahhāb* [the Bestower], which means the One who gives without being asked; *al-Fattāḥ* [the Opener], which means the One who opens the treasuries of His mercy for all His servants; *al-Wāḥid* [the One], He in whose Essence there is no multiplicity; *al-Aḥad* [the Unique], the One who can neither be divided nor qualified; *al-Ṣamad* [the Self-Sustaining], the One to whom everyone turns for the fulfilment of all their wishes.

Note that invocation using all these Names and their subsidiaries should be with *sukūn* [that is, with no vowel] following the last consonant.

Occupy yourself in this station with *al-Fattāḥ* or *al-Wahhāb,* together with *al-Ḥayy,* to ease your progress to the sixth station, of which you are in dire need.

Chapter Six

The Soul Found Pleasing: Its wayfaring, world, location, state, wārid, *attributes, and how to enter upon the seventh Station*

Its wayfaring is 'from' God the Exalted.
Its world is the visible world.
Its location is the Hidden.
Its state is perplexity.
Its *wārid* is transcendence [*tanzīh*].

Its attributes are: goodness of character, forsaking everything other than God the Exalted, gentleness with other human beings, leading them to righteousness, forgiving their misdeeds, loving them and feeling an inclination toward them to take them from the obscurities of their natural egotistic tendencies to their illumined spirits. It is the attribute of this soul to unite [attending to] both creation and Creator; this is a strange thing and is only for those in this sixth station. This is why, in this station, the wayfarer does not appear outwardly different from the common people. Inwardly, however, he is the very essence of secrets and the exemplar of the best of people.

This soul is called 'Found Pleasing' because the Real Himself is pleased with it. The meaning of its wayfaring being 'from' God the Exalted is that it has obtained what it needed from the Divine presence.

Its state is perplexity, but this is a perplexity that is acceptable, similar to that mentioned in the *ḥadīth*: 'Lord, increase my perplexity in You!', not the blameworthy kind which occurs at the beginning of the journey.

It is the attribute of the wayfarer in this station to keep his promises and allocate everything to its proper place. He thus spends liberally when appropriate, to the extent that the ignorant man may think him a profligate, and he may withhold little sums when he thinks it inappropriate to give, so that the ignorant man may think him to be more miserly than all misers. It is his attribute to take the middle course in all his affairs, that which lies between excess and deficiency: and this is something that only the perfect are able to do.[46]

Know that at the beginning of this station the wayfarer shows the first signs of the Greater Vicegerency [*al-Khilāfa al-Kubrā*], and at its end he is invested with it. This is the investiture of 'I am his hearing with which he hears, his sight with which he sees, his hand with which he strikes, and his foot with which he walks.'[47] It is by the Real that he hears, by Him that he sees, by Him that he strikes, and by Him that he walks. This is the consequence of the nearness reached through supererogatory practices and it is for the servant to possess the ability with the Real's help. (Transcendent is He!) Beware of misunderstanding this and believing that the Real either penetrates into anything or is penetrated by anything.

The realization of this station is that when the wayfarer reaches the station of extinction, which is the one previous to this, his reprehensible human qualities, which are the cause of his reactions and wretchedness, are annihilated due to his seeking God's nearness through supererogatory practices, which are the self-discipline and effort which constitute the greater *jihād*. His Lord then, in His Generosity, bestows upon him the attributes which are the opposite of these, arising by leave of their Giver, and this is the Truth of Certainty. And beware of following the path of those who have strayed, for our Lord is too exalted either to be located in anything or for anything to be located in Him. The truth is that these matters lie beyond the reach of reason, unless by Divine grace, for there is nothing external that resembles extinction to serve to demonstrate it.

The same applies to subsistence in God and to the nearness brought about by supererogatory practices.

Hold firmly to *sharīʿa* and occupy yourself with the sixth Name which is *al-Qayyūm* [the Sustainer]. It means the One who is constantly sustaining creation and running its affairs. Maintain the courtesies of both *sharīʿa* and *ṭarīqa*, and let neither one distract you from the other until you reach the seventh Station.

Chapter Seven

The Perfect Soul: its wayfaring, world, location, state, wārid, *and attributes*

Its wayfaring is 'by' God.

Its world is multiplicity in unity and unity in multiplicity.

Its location is the Most Hidden, the relation between it and the Hidden being similar to that of the spirit to the body.

Its state is Subsistence [*baqā'*].

Its *wārid* is all the previously mentioned praiseworthy attributes of the soul.

In this seventh station, occupy yourself with the Name *Qahhār* [Compeller]. This denotes the One who imposes His wishes on creation without resistance.

Know that the one who is in this station has no desire other than the good pleasure of his Lord. His movements are acts of goodness, his every breath is an act of worship. When people see him they are reminded of God - and how else can it be when he is God's perfect saint? He was already a saint when in the fourth station. (Transcendent is He Who when He grants something none can withhold it, and when He withholds something none can grant it!)

The man in this station is constantly worshipping, either with his whole body, or with his tongue, or with his heart. He asks for forgiveness in abundance, and is intensely humble. His joy and delight are in [seeing] created beings turn toward the Real. His sorrow and anger are in [seeing] them turn away from

Him. He loves the seeker of truth more than he loves his own child. He is full of pains, weak in his body and movements. There is no hatred in his heart for any creature at all; however, he still shows aversion where aversion is deserved. He fears no-one when speaking for God. His desire is that of the Real and his Lord immediately answers all his pleas.

Afterword

Know that the Khalwatīs' name is derived from the word *khalwa* [seclusion in a spiritual retreat].[48] They were thus named, despite the fact that all other *ṭarīqas* also practise *khalwa,* because they do it more frequently than the others. The reason for this is the abundance of lights, knowledge, and gnosis that they found in it. Some of them remain in it until their death, others enter it many times every year, others once a year. There are conditions and courtesies to be observed, as Sayyidī Muṣṭafā al-Bakrī[49] mentions in his book *Hadiyyat al-Aḥbāb* [*Gift to the Beloved Ones*]. Its minimum period is three days; it has no maximum, and its optimum is forty days. One of its conditions is that those who wish to practise it should train themselves in self-discipline prior to entering it. [This should involve] hunger, night vigils, isolation,[50] and constant remembrance, so that when they enter it they are already familiar with these and not likely to be repelled by them. Another condition is to intend to enter it in order to detach oneself from the world and concentrate solely upon God. Yet another is that they must feel that they are lowlier than the lowliest of people, lowlier than the sinners, let alone the virtuous, so that God may accept them, for God is with the broken-hearted.[51] Still another condition is to refrain from asking anything at all from God during the retreat, whether it be worldly or other-worldly, but only to worship Him.

Know that the Khalwatīs, as others in the Muḥammadan *ṭarīqas*, are all related to al-Junayd, may God be pleased with him, for he is the 'Master of the Group'. Every *ṭarīqa* then branches into different *ṭarīqas* according to the number of great shaykhs who have mastered it and taken upon themselves the tasks of guidance and the composition of *awrād*.

The Khalwatīs, like the Naqshbandīs, are best known in Turkey, Syria and India. The Shādhilīs and the Qādirīs are better known in the Maghrib. They share a common origin, as we have just said, and they are all agreed that it is necessary to possess determination, expend effort, forsake laziness, remain dissatisfied with oneself, avoid pursuing one's appetites and habits, and maintain constant *dhikr*. Sayyidī Muṣṭafā al-Bakrī,[49] may God be pleased with him, says: 'The first person in the Khalwatī chain [*silsila*] to be given this appellation was the illustrious practising scholar, my brother Muḥammad al-Bālisī,[52] who, because of his exceedingly numerous retreats [*khalwas*] was called "the Khalwatī". The name then extended to his followers who became known as the Khalwatīs and ramified into several branches.'

Know that the sign of the Khalwatīs is the investiture with the common *Khirqa,* which is the 'crown' worn on the head, a round cap of white wool to indicate wayfaring along the path of Sufism and whiteness of the heart. It is embroidered in a special manner and surrounded by four *Jalālas* to indicate that the Lord surrounds his servant from all directions and to indicate independence through God, as in *Wheresoever you turn, there is the Face of God.* [2:115] Some of them leave its centre blank to indicate extinction, and some use the sign 'o' in the centre to indicate the Essence that encompasses the world with knowledge, ability and sustenance, but not in any physical manner. Some place a button in the centre to indicate *Tawḥīd*; others place three buttons on top of each other to indicate the *Tawḥīd* of the Names, Attributes, and Essence; still others draw beneath the button four velvet circles which are either black, red, green, or white, to indicate the four emblems of the Rifāʿīs, Aḥmadīs, Qādirīs, and Dasūqīs according to what each of these spiritual poles [*aqṭāb*] was known to wear. Otherwise the four *Khirqas* are ancient and traceable to the Prophet, may God's blessings and peace be upon him, and they indicate the four deaths: the black death, the red death, and so on.[53] Furthermore, the Khalwatīs wind around their 'crown' a black turban to indicate nobility, mastery and firm foundations, for black is stable and does not change. Sayyidī Aḥmad al-Rifāʿī, may God be pleased with him, is known to have worn it, but it is [ultimately] connected to the master of all creation, may God's blessings and peace be upon him, for his turban was black, as is stated in the *Shamā'il*[54] and other books. The same applies to the other *khirqas*. The Sufi *khirqas* are quite numerous. The emblem of some is a patched robe, that of others the turban, or other items of clothing [which have now gone out of use]. Some invest their disciples with a shirt, others with a *jubba*,[53] this being the special *khirqa* which indicates that he is to wear the robe of the Muḥammadan Succession [*khilāfa*] after his shaykh. Some have crowns that are different from the ones we have just described; such [for instance] is the Wafā'ī *khirqa*,[56] which is accompanied by a white shawl bearing a symbol indicating absorption in the perfection of [Divine] Beauty.

The conditions set by the People for wearing the *khirqa* are wayfaring and permission to wear it from the shaykhs. As for wearing it simply to gratify one's wish, it profits nothing; on the contrary, it is a sign of having strayed, since its indication that one has become a man of God is nothing but a false claim. This does happen to many who claim they are *fuqarā'*;[57] they meet with many others who possess signs, *khirqas*, and special kinds of clothes, they take their oath of allegiance and thus claim affiliation to Sayyidī Aḥmad al-Badawī,[58] Sayyidī Ibrāhīm al-Dasūqī,[59] or others. They may even use this as a trap to gain other people's money on false pretences. They would say, for instance: 'I am an Aḥmadī',[60] which is a lie, since it is a condition, in order to be affiliated to an *imām*, to know his method, behave accordingly, and acquire the courteous qualities that he himself had possessed. However, should they wear their *khirqa* for its *baraka*, refrain from imposing on other people, and make no claims, neither outward nor inward, it is to be hoped that they shall receive some of their *baraka*. This is why a certain gnostic once observed: 'The *khirqa* of the People is, for those who are worthy of it, a light and an adornment, whereas for others it is fatuousness and darkness.'

O God! We beg You to bestow upon us excellence in
courtesy [*adab*], conformity with the Qur'ān and
the *sunna* of Your merciful and compassionate
Prophet, and remoteness from the ego and
the accursed devil, by the honour of the
Prophet, may God's blessings
and peace be upon him!

āmīn

TRANSLATOR'S NOTES

All dates conform to the Muslim calendar

1. The body's 'outward' aspect consists of the physical organs of sensation and locomotion, while the body's 'inward' in this context is the mind.

2. *I claim not that my soul was innocent, indeed the soul incites to evil, except inasmuch as my Lord has mercy.* [12:53]

3. Qur'ānic reference: *I swear by the Day of Arising! And I swear by the reproachful soul!* [75:1,2]

4. The World of Sanctity is the world of Divine matters, the world of transcendence.

5. Qur'ānic reference: *By the soul and That which shaped it, and inspired it with its dissolution and its piety.* [91:7,8]

6. All three terms are derived from the following Qur'ānic passage: *O serene soul, return to your Lord, contented and found pleasing! Join My servants, and enter into My garden.* [89:27]

7. 'Of men many have reached perfection, but of women only four: Āsiya the wife of Pharaoh; Maryam the daughter of ʿImrān; Khadīja the daughter of Khuwaylid; and Fāṭima the daughter of Muḥammad,' says a *ḥadīth*. When perfection is attributed to a created being it is relative, for absolute perfection can belong only to the One, the Infinite. In the case of the finite, its perfection consists in its uniting in itself the attributes whose possession amounts to perfection for him and similar kinds of beings. In this particular context perfection means the completion of the journey and the completion of the attributes whose possession amounts to saintly perfection. These attributes will be possessed to a greater or lesser degree of fullness, and there will therefore be perfect or complete saints who are more perfect or complete than others. Divine gifts are infinitely varied, and as God is the Unique, each of His gifts is also unique. Each person of God is therefore unique since each receives Openings that are exclusively his or hers.

8. The four 'elements' originate in the primordial substance called *hāyūlā*. They are air, earth, water and fire. Neither the primordial substance nor the elements are to be understood in a material sense; rather they are

the non-material origin of matter, each of the elements being given the name of the material element that most corresponds to it in its attributes.

9. Being the nearest to the Absolute, the Prophet, *ṣalla'Llāhu ʿalayhi wa-sallam*, is the nearest created being to absolute perfection. This is why the outpouring of Divine mercy from God toward creation is concentrated on him and radiates from him to pervade all the degrees of existence. And this is what is meant by the expression *ṣalla'Llāhu ʿalayhi*, translated as 'may God's blessings be upon him'. As for *wa-sallam*, which means 'and peace be upon him', it is the ability to receive this influx of Divine lights yet remain firm and serene. To use Sufi terminology, the element of 'blessings' leads to extinction (*fanā'*) or intoxication (*sukr*), while the element 'peace' leads to subsistence (*baqā'*) or sobriety (*sahw*), and mastery (*tamkīn*).

10. Following the breathing of the Divine Spirit into the Adamic form, God commanded the angels to prostrate themselves before Adam, who thus became their *qibla*. They were in effect prostrating before the Divine mystery within Adam and acknowledging that he was the *khalīfa* or vicegerent. If the *Kaʿba*, which is the material *qibla*, corresponds to Adam's body, the Muḥammadan Reality (*al-ḥaqīqa al-Muḥammadiyya*), which is the *qibla* of pure spirits, corresponds to the Spirit within Adam.

11. Abū Hurayra was the most prolific narrator of *ḥadīth* among the Companions, the Prophet having prayed for him that God should strengthen his memory so that he would forget nothing of what he heard from him. One of the Ahl al-Ṣuffa, he died in the year 57.

12. ʿAbdallāh ibn Masʿūd: a scholarly Companion and narrator of *ḥadīth*. He died in the year 32.

13. The root of the Arabic term for ignorance is *j-h-l*. *Jahl* is ignorance itself, while the ignorant man is *jāhil*, and the pre-Islamic Age of Ignorance is the *Jāhiliyya*. However, the meaning also includes some of the consequences of ignorance, and is therefore used to imply bad temper, arrogant or injurious behaviour, and prejudice of any kind. A well-known prayer of the Prophet, to be recited prior to leaving one's house, requests God's protection from both treating others with ignorance or being so treated by them.

14. ʿAlī ibn Abī Ṭālib: The Blessed Prophet's cousin and son-in-law, and the first male Muslim. His martial prowess became legendary and he was to be the fourth Rightly-guided Caliph. He was martyred in the year 40 of the Hijra.

15. ʿAbdallāh ibn ʿUmar: A leading scholar, *ḥadīth* narrator and *muftī* among the Companions, he was the son of the second Caliph. He died in the year 74.

16. Balʿam ibn Bāʿūrā: A Hebrew rabbi said by some commentators to have been meant by the following Qur'ānic passage: *And recite to them the tiding of him to whom We gave Our signs, but he cast them off, and the Devil followed after him, and he became one of those led astray.* [7:176]

17. Ibrāhīm ibn Adham: An early Sufi, the first of the great ones mentioned by Qushayrī in his *Risāla*. He was a prince who renounced his kingdom and lived as a wandering ascetic until his death in Syria. He died in the year 161.

18. Muʿādh ibn Jabal. One of the most dynamic and learned of the companions of the Prophet, may Allah bless him and grant him peace. He died in the year 18.

19. Abū Bakr al-Ṣiddīq. The first man to accept the call to Islam, the Blessed Prophet's close companion throughout the years of his mission and his first successor as head of the new Islamic state. He died in the year 13 of the Hijra.

20. The miraculous Night Journey comprised two stages, the *Isrā'* and the *Miʿrāj*. The first describes the Blessed Prophet's 'night journey' from Makka to Jerusalem. During the course of the second, the Prophet's Ascension through the seven heavens, the Prophet was shown the torments of the damned in hell, and described them in great detail to his Companions on his return.

21. ʿĀ'isha. The youngest of the Prophet's wives and Abū Bakr's daughter, she was to become, after the Prophet's death, one of the leading scholars of Islam, and was the major channel of transmission for his teachings concerning the affairs of Muslim women. She died in the year 58.

22. Yūsuf al-Siddīq: the Prophet Joseph, may peace be upon him. Abraham's great-grandson who became Egypt's governor and caused the Hebrews to emigrate into Egypt. Zulaykhā, the wife of al-ʿAzīz, caused Joseph's imprisonment when he resisted her advances, then after his release accepted his religion and became his wife.

23. *Ṭabʿ* and *khatm* are almost synonymous. The first means 'to stamp' and the second 'to seal'. God says, *And a seal has been set upon their hearts, so they understand not* [8:87], and *Those are they upon whose hearts God has set a seal, and they have followed their caprices.* [47:16]

24. *Rayn* is that which covers, as rust covers a sword or as wine covers the mind. It results from the accumulation of the effects of deviant beliefs and sins on the heart so as to render it blind.

25. The Arabic term used is *yugharghir,* from a verb meaning 'to gurgle', and refers here to the death rattle.

26. Abū ʿAbdallāh Muḥammad al-Sanūsī of Tlemçen in Algeria (d.895). Author of five well-known summaries of Islamic doctrine: *al-Kubrā*, *al-Wusṭā*, *al-Ṣughrā*, *Ṣughrā al-Ṣughrā*, and *al-Muqaddima*. The *Ṣughrā* is also known as *Umm al-Barāhīn*. With the commentary by al-Faḍālī (d.1236) Sanūsī's work is one of the textbooks on theology taught at al-Azhar University in Cairo. Al-Sanūsī was also a noted Sufi.

27. 'That which is God's' is the Afterlife, the Garden and the delight of beholding the Divine Countenance for some, and hell and the torment of remoteness for others.

28. *Indeed those who fear God shall dwell amid gardens and rivers, in a seat of truth in the presence of a Sovereign Omnipotent,* [54:55] that is, in a place where they shall be secure and honoured with the permanent consequences of their past truthfulness and sincerity.

29. Abū Ḥātim Muḥammad ibn Ḥibbān (d.354). *Ḥadīth* scholar who composed a famous collection of sound *ḥadīths, Al-Ṣaḥīḥ.*

30. Ismāʿīl is Ishmael, Abraham's son by Hājar the Egyptian.

31. ʿArafa, or ʿArafāt, is the great plain around the Mount of Mercy, where the Standing (*wuqūf*), the culminating rite of Ḥajj, takes place.

32. The 'Ones Brought Near' (*al-muqarrabūn*) are mentioned in the Holy Qur'ān [56:11, 83:21]. They are the highest ranks of the pure-hearted, and thus are higher than ordinary good believers, the People of the Right Hand (*aṣḥāb al-yamīn*).

33. *Assuredly in the creation of the heavens and the earth and in the alternation of night and day there are signs for possessors of cores. Those who remember God, standing and sitting and on their sides, and reflect upon the creation of the heavens and the earth.* [3:190-1] Those possessed of a 'core', or *lubb*, are those who have reached the stage where their remembrance of God is unbroken and they are seldom forgetful of their Lord, whatever they may be doing. Only then are they able to recognise the signs in the creation of the heavens and earth as signs, that is, as indicators of higher realities and ultimately of the Highest Reality of all, which is the Absolute. As for minds which lack this kind of concentration and are suffering from the dispersion caused by their numerous attachments to the world, they are rarely able to recognise these Divine indicators for what they are and, furthermore, deny others the ability to do so; not content with being blind they also wish to impose their blindess on the rest of humanity.

34. This is a reference to the *ḥadīth* cited previously (p.21) which enjoins those Muslims capable of understanding this to remember God until the others accuse them of being mad; mad, that is, because they are forgetful of their worldly interests and concentrate on their afterlife; or in other words, prefer the inward to the outward, which is inconceivable for profane people.

35. This is because prior to receiving the Opening, one is incapable of the kind of profound spiritual discernment that is needed for safety on the path, whereas after the Opening the gnostic is able to look back, recognise his shortcomings, and strive to remedy them before rising to the next station. In other words, once he comes into direct conscious contact with his own highest reality, he becomes, to a greater or lesser extent depending on his rank, his own guide.

36. *There is no creature that walks but that He takes it by the forelock. Indeed my Lord is on a straight path.* [11:56]

37. *By the soul and That which shaped it, and inspired it with its dissolution and its piety.* [91:7,8]

38. *We indeed created man in the fairest stature, then We restored him as lowest of the low. Save those who believe, and do righteous works.* [95:4-6] The 'fairest stature' is the primordial Adamic nature of mankind, and one must remember that Adam was no less than a Prophet, may peace be upon him. It is also the state of the spirit prior to its entry into this world, the world of corruption. When God appeared to the gathered spirits and asked them, 'Am I not your Lord?' they all answered, 'Yea!' since they could not deny what they were actually beholding. The 'lowest of the low', on the other hand, is the condition of total denial of these realities by the spirits once they become veiled by bodies and their baser drives. Between the 'fairest stature' and the 'lowest of the low' are the innumerable degrees separating bestial from perfect man, which the author has reduced, for the sake of intelligibility, to the seven stations he describes.

39. This world and the next.

40. A master must sometimes test his disciple's sincerity, determination, and trustworthiness. The greater the spiritual stature of the disciple the more extreme the form of the test, since it is the great disciples who will be entrusted with the Divine secrets. *We offered the trust to the heavens and the earth and the mountains,* says the Qur'ān, *but they refused to carry it and were afraid of it, and man carried it.* [33:79]

41. Abu'l-Qāsim al-Junayd. The 'Master of the Group', a scholar of *fiqh* and one of the greatest exponents of Sufism, which he received from al-Sarī al-Saqaṭī. He lived and taught in Baghdad, where he died in 298.

42. *Al-Ḥikam* is a famous collection of Sufi aphorisms widely read in Sufi circles all over the Islamic world. Its importance is demonstrated by the number of masters who wrote commentaries on it. Its author is Shaykh Ibn ʿAṭā'illāh of Alexandria (d.709), who was the third shaykh of the Shādhilī *ṭarīqa,* after its founder, the great imām Abu'l-Ḥasan al-Shādhilī, and his successor Shaykh Abu'l-ʿAbbās al-Mursī. Besides his renown as a Sufi, the shaykh was also an authoritative scholar and one of the most eminent teachers at Al-Azhar University. An English version of the work exists, translated by Victor Danner as *The Book of Wisdom*, SPCK, London 1979 (1399).

43. Bishr ibn al-Ḥārith al-Ḥāfī. The great 'barefoot' Sufi of Baghdad known for his scrupulousness and circumspection in religious matters. A companion of the *walī* al-Fuḍayl ibn ʿIyāḍ, he died in the year 227.

44. Divine retaliation may seem, at first sight, somewhat disproportionate in this story, compared with the offence committed. However, God says in the *ḥadīth qudsī,* 'Whosoever is hostile to a friend [*walī*] of Mine I declare war on him.' (Bukhārī.) An attack on a man of God is considered by God to be an attack on Him and He retaliates accordingly. The culprit in this story must have known that the man he was casting stones at was a saint, that is, a Friend of God, and his crime is therefore one of *lesé majesté.* This is why God hides His Friends from profane eyes under an apparently

mundane appearance, out of mercy for those ignorant enough to abuse them verbally or attack them physically, for if they do so unaware that they are saints then the crime is no more than that of one Muslim abusing another, and its punishment does not exceed that which is stated in *sharīʿa*.

45. See Qur'ān 12:54.

46. In a *ḥadīth* we read: 'The best of matters is the middle course.' To be extreme is easy; to find the middle way demands wisdom and intelligence; hence it is the aspect of the man or woman who has purified the soul to this high degree.

47. In the famous *ḥadīth* narrated by Imām al-Bukhārī we read: 'Whoever is hostile to a *walī* [saint/friend] of Mine, I declare war on him. My bondsman draws near to Me with nothing dearer to Me than what I have imposed upon him. My bondsman continues to draw closer to Me until I love him. And when I love him I become the eye with which he sees, the ear with which he hears, the hand with which he strikes, and the foot with which he walks.' See note 44 above.

48. The author, may Allah show him His mercy and illuminate his grave, was an exponent of the Khalwatī *ṭarīqa*, whose emphasis on the sevenfold division of the soul is manifested in this book. The Khalwatiyya are among the most exalted and respected of all Sufi orders in Islam, often being regarded as a *ṭarīqa* for the *ʿulamā'*. In fact, some branches of the Khalwatiyya do not accept initiates for the pledge of loyalty (*bayʿa*) unless they have reached a high level of Islamic learning. Hence, for instance, the present *imām* of the Al-Azhar Mosque, Shaykh Ismāʿīl Ṣādiq al-ʿAdawī, is a Khalwatī. He was previously *imām* of the mosque attached to the tomb of al-Quṭb Aḥmad Dardīr, the great Mālikī and Khalwatī scholar whose book *Tuḥfat al-Ikhwān* (Cairo, 1964CE) describes his inner condition upon attaining each of the seven degrees of the soul. The main practice of the Khalwatiyya is the recitation of the *Wird al-Sattār*, often by a single reciter in the presence of many listeners. This blessed *wird* (litany) has been handed down from Shaykh Yaḥyā Shirwānī, may Allah sanctify his secret, who lived in Azerbaijān and died in 869. It is a *wird* which celebrates the unity of Allah, and praises the Blessed Prophet and his Companions, and has been commented on at length by Shaykh ʿUmar al-Shabrāwī. Branches of the Khalwatiyya active today include the Shabrāwiyya and Damīrdāshiyya in Egypt, the Jarrāḥiyya of Istanbul, and the Sammāniyya, founded in Makka but today concentrated in the Sudan.

49. A leading reformist figure of the Khalwatī ṭarīqa, Muṣṭafā ibn Kamāl al-Bakrī was born in Damascus in 1099 and died in Cairo in 1162. He was a pupil of ʿAbd al-Ghanī al-Nablusī, whose teachings are manifest in his didactic poem *Bulghat al-Murīd*, and in his book *al-Mawrid al-ʿAdhb*, in which al-Bakrī outlines the orthodox understanding of the doctrine of the Unity of Being (*waḥdat al-wujūd*), a teaching which had been misinterpreted by many. His famous book of prayers and *awrād*, *Majmūʿ Ṣalawāt wa-*

awrād, was printed in Cairo in 1308. His main textbook on Khalwatī practice is *al-Waṣiyya al-Jalīla li'l-sālikīn ṭarīqat al-Khalwatiyya*, which has not yet been printed.

50. Isolation (*ʿuzla*) is not the same as retreat (*khalwa*). The first implies keeping away from the common people in general except for attending the five prayers, whereas the second requires total seclusion for a determined period, under special conditions.

51. 'I am with those whose hearts break for My sake,' says God in a *ḥadīth qudsī*.

52. Muḥammad ibn Nūr al-Bālisī was the true founder of the Khalwatī ṭarīqa, and the shaykh of the ʿUmar al-Khalwatī who died in Tabrīz in the year 800.

53. According to Jurjānī, death is an existential attribute created to be the opposite of life. In the technical language of the people of Truth it is to suppress the ego's whims. The one who suppresses his whims lives with His guidance. The 'Red Death' is the opposition to the ego. The 'White Death' is hunger, because it illuminates the inward and whitens the face of the heart. He whose gluttony dies, his perspicacity comes alive. The 'Green Death' is to wear patched rags, worthless and discarded by others. His life is verdant with contentment. The 'Black Death' is the endurance of harm from others. It is to be extinct in God and witness harm as coming from him by perceiving all acts as the Act of the Beloved. (Al-Sharīf ʿAlī ibn Muḥammad al-Jurjānī, *Kitāb al-Taʿrīfat* (Cairo, 1306).) At a deeper level some Sufis regard the four colours as indicating the four levels of existence and consequently the four levels of *tawḥīd*. Shaykh Bursevī quotes the following story in his Qur'ānic commentary: 'It is said that a *walī* known as Sukkānī Bābā had times when he was so utterly absorbed that people thought him dead [...] One day he awoke from that state, declaring that he was intent on divorcing his wife and leaving his children. "I was at a session with the Prophet, may peace be upon him," he said, "in the *malakūt*, with the spirits, while the Prophet, may peace be upon him, was explaining God's saying *and your God is but a single God,* [2:163] and discoursing on the levels of *tawḥīd*, sitting on a chair the four legs of which were of the four lights corresponding to the four levels. These were: of black light at the level of [physical] nature, of red light at the level of the soul, of green light at the level of the spirit, and of white light at the level of the Secret. Then it was said at the Throne: 'Let Sukkānī Bābā go, for his children are weeping!' This is why I want to leave everyone." The family promised they would not disturb him again and he relented.' (Ismāʿīl Ḥaqqī Bursevī (d.1137), *Tafsīr Rūḥ al-Bayān*, repr. Beirut 1405, II, 331.)

54. The *Shamā'il* (Perfect Qualities) probably referred to here is the *ḥadīth* collection of this name by al-Tirmidhī (d.279).

55. A *jubba* is a long robe, which may take various forms.

56. The Wafā'ī *ṭarīqa* is mainly found in Syria and Egypt.

57. *Fuqarā'*: those who recognise the Qur'ānic saying: *O mankind! You are the poor before God, and God is the Rich, the Owner of praise.* (35:15) In some traditions of Sufism, a life of poverty may be required at certain stages of the Path, to strip away the ego's attachment to the things of this world.

58. Sayyidī Aḥmad al-Badawī (d.675) was a Ḥusaynī sayyid who was born in Fez, grew up in Makka, and spent his last forty years in the Nile Delta town of Ṭanṭā, where he founded one of the major Sufi orders, the Aḥmadiyya.

59. Ibrāhīm al-Dassūqī (d.646). A Ḥusaynī sayyid who lived and died in Dassūq in the north of Egypt. He was a born lover of God, and founded a great Sufi order.

60. An Aḥmadī here means a follower of Sayyidī Aḥmad al-Badawī (see note 58 above).

INDEX